Moonra

Moonraking

by

A. G. STREET

illustrated by

LIONEL EDWARDS, R.I.

OXFORD UNIVERSITY PRESS

1988

Oxford University Press, Walton Street, Oxford OX2 6DP

Oxford New York Toronto
Delhi Bombay Calcutta Madras Karachi
Petaling Jaya Singapore Hong Kong Tokyo
Nairobi Dar es Salaam Cape Town
Melbourne Auckland

and associated companies in
Berlin Ibadan

Oxford is a trade mark of Oxford University Press

First published 1936 by Eyre & Spottiswoode Ltd.
First issued as an Oxford University Press paperback 1988

British Library Cataloguing in Publication Data
Street, A. G. (Arthur George). 1892–1966
Moonraking.
1. England. Agriculture. Street, A. G. (Arthur George), 1892–1966. Biographies
I. Title
630'.92'4
ISBN 0-19-282219-5

Library of Congress Cataloging in Publication Data
Street, A. G. (Arthur George), 1892–1966.
Moonraking/by A. G. Street; illustrated by Lionel Edwards.   p. cm.
Reprint. Originally published: London: Eyre and Spottiswoode, 1936.
1. Street, A. G. (Arthur George), 1892–1966—Biography. 2. Authors,
English—20th century—Biography. 3. Farmers—England—
Wiltshire—Biography. 4. Farm life—England—Wiltshire.
5. Wiltshire—Social life and customs. I. Title.
630'.92'4—dc19   PR6037.T7762465 1988   [B]   88-4216
ISBN 0-19-282219-5

Printed in Great Britain by
The Guernsey Press Co. Ltd.
Guernsey, Channel Islands

Foreword

Like my father before me, I was brought up on the legend of the Wiltshire Moonrakers: how, in the seventeenth century, one night when a full moon was shining down on the little village of Bishops Cannings, a few local inhabitants were engaged in smuggling some kegs of brandy, carefully concealed beneath a wagon-load of hay. On hearing the sound of horses' hooves, they hastily extricated their illicit goods and dumped them in a conveniently placed pond. The excisemen who arrived on the scene searched the cart and rode away but, evidently still suspicious, quietly doubled back on their tracks where they found the smugglers performing the curious task of trying to recover the booty with their hay-rakes. When asked what they thought they were up to, one of the culprits, with admirable presence of mind, pointed to the splendid reflection of the moon in the water and said, "Zomebody 'ave lost thic thur cheese and we'm a-rakin' for 'un in thic thur pond." The excisemen smiled and went on their way to Devizes, having been completely fooled by these simple rustics—as they thought them—who had so successfully pretended to be fools themselves.

In his Introduction to *Moonraking*, my father refers to some initial doubts about his choice of title, partly because "moon" was so often associated with insanity and, while though not insane, he wondered whether the "rakings" of a mind such as his would be worth anything. The fact that over half a century later—in keeping with its earlier com-

Foreword

panion volume, *Country Calendar*—these rakings are being republished seems proof enough of their worth.

Rereading both books today brings back infinitely precious and vivid memories of my youth; but judging by the response to *Country Calendar* when it was reissued in paperback by Oxford University Press in 1986, as well as *Farmer's Glory* in 1983, it would appear that I, who have every reason to derive pleasure from his writing, am by no means alone in appreciating how well it has stood up to the passage of time. His enjoyment of life, love of the land, interest in all that went on around him and, above all, his common sense and humanity seem to come over with the same impact in the 1980s as they did in the 1930s.

My father was a great believer in the importance of "keeping on keeping on". That there are now three of his books still in print doing just that, seems a splendid testimony to such a maxim.

PAMELA STREET

London, 1988

Contents

List of Illustrations

List of Illustrations

Introduction

I have often wondered just when an introduction to a book should be written. Should one write the book first, and then, having discovered what it is about, write a suitable introduction ? Or should one write the introduction first, and then struggle for months to make some seventy thousand odd words sing in tune with the chosen keynote ? Or is it wisest and safest to dispense with any introduction, on the arrogant assumption that a good wine needs no bush ?

Most people, I feel sure, would vote for the last method, and usually I should agree with them ; but for this book I must have an introduction, and I must write it before I begin. The reason is that generally when I begin a book, although I will admit that the major portion of its contents are a completely unknown quantity, I do know just when and how it is going to end. But in this case I have no notion of either the beginning, the middle, or the end. Consequently, I have racked my brains for hours in search of a suitable title for something so hazy, thinking that unless this were found, the book could never be even begun ; and then, having found this necessary thing, I discovered that without some explanation my choice would be misleading to most readers.

In one sense " Moonraking " is an apt enough title, for the old smuggling legend has left the name " Moonraker " as a legacy to all Wiltshiremen. " Moonraking," therefore, must surely refer to the musings of a Moonraker ; but, although I am a Wiltshire Moonraker, born and bred, I find nowadays that my mental raking is not confined to Wiltshire's mellow fields. Although I still farm some of them, circumstances which are neither my fault nor my misfortune compel me to rake in all sorts of queer places, in both town and country, and all over this green island.

For this reason I was tempted at first to discard " Moonraking " as being unsuitable and misleading, but after a while its peculiar aptness dawned upon me. With the latter half of the word no one could pick a quarrel, and surely " Moon " is very applicable to my present mental condition ? For the moon has always been associated with insanity ; and, even if I am not insane as the world reads the word, my mind is in a most horrible muddle.

How can it be otherwise ? One day a farmer ; the next an author ; the next—God forgive me—a lecturer at a university ; then back to farming ; next deserting the fresh air of Wilts for the peculiar atmosphere of Broadcasting House ; then a journalist ; next perhaps feeling like a fish out of water at a London cocktail party ; then discovering at my club that some of this country's most famous men have such delightfully coarse minds that a Wiltshire farmer feels quite at home in their company ; next in grave consultation with some of our rulers concerning agricultural policy, wondering all the time just how and why I should be present, and knowing full well that whatever is decided in Whitehall the grass won't grow until the rain comes ; then lunching with a publisher ; perhaps drinking (in strict moderation) with an editor ; but ever and anon returning to my Wiltshire farm and recognizing that it is the one stable thing in my uncertain, kaleidoscopic and peripatetic life. Can it be doubted that once in a while I do not know whether I am on my head or my heels, that I am moonstruck, and that " Moonraking " is the most suitable title for this book ?

Will the rakings of such a bewildered mind as mine be worth anything ? I wonder. Children and fools are supposed to speak the truth ; and, if truth be told, most adults, even moonstruck ones, think the truth at some time or another. For myself I find that truth comes to me when I do not definitely set out to seek it, and generally at two especial times of my usual day. One is during those few delightful moments before sleep, and the other whilst I am lying blissfully soaking in a hot bath. During these times of delicious privacy I find that I attain complete honesty of mind. It is comparatively easy to be honest with other people—in fact such a procedure usually pays— but how difficult it is to be honest with oneself ! But as I approach the frontiers of sleep, or whilst I gravely contemplate the pink contours of my big toe as it rides like a mark buoy amidst the steamy rack of bathdom, I tell myself the truth about myself and everything and everybody with whom I have come into contact.

Rightly or wrongly I consider that these honest thoughts of mine are worthy to fill the following book, but I am well aware that to rake them together will be no easy task. To turn back from sleep to waking, to light the light, and to commit any of them to paper is too much to expect from tired middle-age. At such moments sleep is far too attractive a country. So, that film story which would have brought me affluence, that rural play which would have run for several years, that novel which would have been acclaimed as a classic, and that wonderful agricultural policy which would have brought prosperity to both town and country

Past and present

can never be written ; for memory invariably refuses to recall them next morning.

Perhaps it is just as well. Were either to happen I might be forced to live in town ? Perish the thought ! Let us turn to the lonely narrows of the bath ; where every man is honest, and every woman lovely ; where naked truth is very pleasant, and naked beauty brings no blush. In this harbour I must keep awake or drown, and so the results of my mental raking there shall be found stacked between the covers of this book. For, mark you, it is possible to keep a pencil and pad upon the soap rack.

" In Autumn, when the leaves are brown,
Take pen and ink and write it down"

Holiday Time

For the same reason that no farmer should have a motor car no farmer should ever take a holiday. Either happening is considered by the majority of towsnfolk as proof positive that food is much too dear. Why this should be, I cannot quite make out. Surely a man who works an average of sixty hours weekly the year through and who in addition has several thousand pounds of his own capital invested in his business, is more entitled to take a holiday than the thousands of salaried folk who have none of their own capital at risk, and the comfortable expectation of a pension in old age ? For I am very conscious that the average farmer can claim no holidays at full pay by legal right ; that he can take only those holidays for which he can afford to pay ; and that unless he provides for his own pension he will have to whistle for it.

So, to give the initial chapter of this book such a title as " Holiday Time " is asking for it, and doubtless the future will see that I get it in good measure. Besides, while a farmer may possibly escape public censure for taking a holiday, the reviews of my last note-book told me very plainly that a farmer-writer cannot do so. From them I gathered that as long as my pen is kept well dipped in the mud of my farm work all is well ; but that my occasional refills at the fountain of rural sport and pleasure are anything but.

In one sense I recognize the justice of these strictures. Most people are most interesting when they are talking or

writing of their work ;   and I know full well, while the joys
of golf, fishing, riding, shooting, and other country pleasures
are familiar to the multitude, that the intimate particulars
of every day life on a farm are news to them.   But surely all
work and no play would make both Jack and Jack's book
rather dull, and on that ground may I be permitted to use
a little of the latter as a leaven ?   Anyway here goes, and
chance the ducks.

*   *   *   *   *   *

A small acreage of corn and an early harvest have combined to enable me to take a holiday in late August, a thing
which has not come my way since childhood.   Such an
opportunity required that fresh ground must be broken, so
to-morrow my family and I are off to the toe of England,
almost to Land's End, for a whole fortnight.

To-day the house has been in the throes of packing—no
place for me anywhere—so I have been farming hard.   It's
queer how difficult it always is for a farmer to leave his farm
for a week or two.   All may look well ;   every possible
contingency may be arranged for ;   one's men may be con-
scientious, efficient, and trustworthy ;   and yet one
worries.   Why ?   Simply because on a farm one never
knows ;   anything may happen, and usually does.   Still,
all farming is one damn risk after another, so one extra
won't make much odds.

To-day I have walked over every field on the farm ;   I
have paid the men for three weeks to come ;   I have seen to
it that there's an ample supply of cake in the barn ;   and,
for once in my life, I have my correspondence up-to-date.
The wheat ricks are thatched ;   the cattle appear to be in the
best of health ;   Charlie, my dairyman and foreman, has
agreed a plan of campaign for wet or fine weather ;   and the

glass is set fair. Barring earthquakes, war, or strikes, it would seem that my presence will not be missed. But like all farmers I expect I shall be fool enough to worry all the time I am away ; which, while it may be natural, is very silly, for think of the thousands of people who have run my farm before me and the thousands who will tend it after I am dead. Men come and go, but the land remains ; any man can be done without, but the land cannot.

So, here's for bed, an early start in the morning, and a carefree holiday. But I think I will take a note-book with me, just in case.

*　　*　　*　　*　　*　　*

Trust a farmer to take a busman's holiday ! Not for me the palatial hotel, but instead a Cornish farmhouse not half-a-dozen miles from Land's End ; and up-to-date, none of our party has anything but praise for the choice. In fact I can whole-heartedly recommend it to anyone ; for, now that so much of England's farming is so planned and mechanized in every detail, a farm like this one is hard to find.

As the setting for a summer holiday it is ideal. It is all that a farm should be. It is the farm of my childhood's memory, the farm of every child's dreams. There is a large stone farmhouse with a higgledy-piggledy range of farm buildings tacked on to it. Pigs, poultry, three cats, a wise sheep-dog aptly named Driver, two red setters less aptly named Rose and Dante, and Nora, a hound bitch puppy of engaging habits and an insatiable appetite, are our intimate companions from the moment we step outside the front door. Indeed, if the lower window of our sitting-room is left open for a moment, Nora and the cats are inside and on the table ; while Driver grins wide approval with his fore paws on the sill. There are cows and horses and ducks and sheep and ferrets and rabbits and tame pigeons seemingly everywhere. And last, but by no means least, there is a most delightful family of human beings as our hosts. What they think of us English foreigners I know not, nor am I fool enough to inquire. But already I must put on record that we are grateful for their kindness and courtesy.

And over all is peace—the peace of Cornish agriculture, which passeth a Wiltshire farmer's understanding, but which he finds all-sufficing while he is on holiday. There is only one word which describes it properly, a modern adjective which is continuously on the lips of one of my young nephews—" swell."

It is more than swell, it is marvellous. Harvest is in full swing. So are dairying, pig-keeping, and many other farming activities ; while in addition to my own family there are other summer visitors staying at this farm. But there is a complete absence of fuss, both on the farm and in the house. Farming and catering are well done without the slightest sign of hurry of worry, and without any regard for law or regulation. Even my car is subdued to the prevailing slow rhythm, for the twists in the lanes and the recumbent swine in the straight portions of them make any speed greater than ten miles per hour impossible.

In case I may be giving the impression that this particular farm is the exception which proves the rule, let me hasten to say that the whole countryside around smiles in similarly peaceful content. Little fields, farmed well according to ancient custom and without the aid of much machinery—such little fields, pocket handkerchiefs, brown most of them owing to the drought, and each with a grey-green hemstitching of stone wall. Sometimes a corn field of but two acres, the crop standing in stook for a week, and then put into high conical mows, perhaps only a half-dozen in the whole field. No snorting tractors, no combine harvesters, no milking machines, and consequently, no noise. Here a patch of corn, there a few yellow Guernsey cows in a brown pasture, and then, by way of contrast, a vivid green square of broccoli. Toy farming, if you like, but it has its points. The corn crops are invariably heavy, the milk is rich, the pork and lamb are tender, and the broccoli has a world-wide reputation. And at night, when the placid progress of it all has ceased for a while, perfect quiet. The whole world seems hushed and still, the only sign of man's activities being the regular flash of the Lizard light across a velvet sky. To quote my modern nephew once more, " It's swell."

*   *   *   *   *   *

Placidity must be catching, for after three or four days of Cornwall I find that I have succumbed to it. A beautiful physical and mental content has come over me. Forgotten is the mechanical bustle of my Wiltshire farm, which goes on daily from before dawn until sunset and often even later ; forgotten are newspapers, wireless, telephones, and all the manifold contrivances by which man has seen to it that his mind shall never rest while he is awake ; and for me that other England of towns and bustle does not exist, save only as a bad dream. I am game to do anything or nothing, whichever may suit my companions ; and they, thanks be, are in like mood. So, drunk with Cornish peace and privacy and colour, we are spending our holiday in lazy and grateful content.

Peace is over all, privacy waits to welcome us in every little cove, and colour is everywhere. The first two

Over all is peace

blessings Cornwall owes to its geographical position. Even in these days of swift transport it is a far cry from our large cities, and its only land approach is from the east. Result, while the eastern three-quarters of our south coast is black with people during summertime, by comparison the most western ten miles of it is only faintly sprinkled with holiday makers. So in most cases we have been able to make the rocks our bathing tent, and this unusual privacy has made me, who am but a poor bather at the best of times, bathe daily with enthusiasm.

For my sins I am one of those who are condemned to drink some of the water in which they bathe. I will admit that my palate, both for wine or water, is an indifferent one, although I can claim to some discrimination in the question of beer. Consequently, I cannot distinguish the subtle differences of flavour which must exist between the blue water at Cadgwith and Kennack, the green water at Sennen and Porth Curnow, and the mauves and purples and golds at St. Ives, Gunwalloe, and many other havens of delight. But this I can say with truth. I have drunk of them all, and can vouch that they are all well worth drinking. Not for thirty years have I gone to bed night after night with sand between my toes.

* * * * * *

I know nothing of painting, and I must confess that most of the work of modern artists gives me a pain in the neck. In addition, I am a Philistine and an ignoramus concerning anything to do with pictures ; and, like most farmers, my interest in them when I do look at them is confined to hunting for any inaccuracy of detail rather than in admiring the general impression. Under this heading may I here be permitted to inquire why it is that so many artists will depict the plough turning the furrow in the opposite direction to the age-old habit of that implement— from right to left instead of from left to right ? Is it because art is considered superior to truth in the eyes of artists, or because they really do see the plough at work like that ? Possibly the latter, for I once heard artists introduced to an audience in this fashion by a friend of mine.

" Ladies and gentleman," he said. " For our sins we have in this club several artists, and some of them now propose to draw something. Artists tell us that they depict life as they see it, and from some of their pictures one gathers that at all events, they do see life."

However, I know that I can trust my friend, Mr. Lionel Edwards, to keep faith with the plough as a true country-man should, so let me get on with these notes.

Somehow or other, I, a farmer, must set down something about Cornwall's colour. What my artist friend,
who lives at Sancreed only a bare mile from this farm, will
say to such audacity, I dare not think. However, I must
risk his displeasure ; for I am drunk with colour. It is
everywhere, all the time. The whole countryside is drenched
with colour, morning, noon, and night. The land is golden,
the seas are glorious, and the skies are glad with it. The
countless differing shades must be seen to be believed ; and
no one who has not seen them should dare to pass criticism
on the artist's attempts to reproduce them on paper or
canvas.

I say that because only this morning I overheard a lady
who was looking into a stationer's window in Penzance say
to her friend, " Just look at those absurd postcards. There
cannot be colour like that in nature. Why must they
overdraw the picture ? "

Evidently she had just arrived on her first visit to
Cornwall, for all the colours in those postcards I have
already seen and admired. No matter where you go in this
district or what the weather it seems that the world is full
of colour, and never once have I come across a dull, grey sea.

*   *   *   *   *   *

In case anyone should think from this eulogy of Cornwall
that I have been bribed by some Cornish business interest
to write only in praise of this part of the world as a setting
for a holiday, let me hasten to set down my adventure of
last night.

Whilst one can obtain the precious boons of quiet and
privacy from a holiday spent in truly rural surroundings,
one is often reminded by their lack that the amenities of the
town have their value. The absence of inside sanitation

and water supply in our present abode has caused my family some heart-searchings ever since we arrived. This is only natural, for I can remember hearing an eminent lecturer, after expatiating for nearly an hour on the blessings of life some fifty years ago, finish up with, " In fact, ladies and gentlemen, there are only two things in modern life which I should regret, were I to be transported back to live in the England of my grandfather. They are the modern bathroom and the modern water closet."

I have a notion that most people would agree with him. Anyway the ladies of my family do so most heartily, and it is the lack of the latter of these essentials to comfort which has most exercised their minds since our arrival. The earthy convenience put at our disposal has no terrors for them during daylight, but they have and are consumed with the awful fear of being constrained to visit it in the night watches. Of course, I pooh-poohed their worryings. I told them they were spoilt by luxury and comfort. I told them lurid stories of Canadian sanitation as practised by the bachelor shanty dwellers of North-West Manitoba. I besought them to take heart by considering me, a man who had lived for years under such conditions in the wide open spaces of the Empire. Surely for one fortnight they could do the same ? I laughed their feminine fears to scorn.

But Fate took a hand last night, and ironically insisted that I should be the first pressed man to brave the lonely dangers of the dark. Possibly that lobster at St. Ives is more to blame than Fate, but anyway at two a.m. I awoke, realizing that the garden must be visited, immediately if not sooner.

Next time I stay at this farmhouse—and please God it may not be long delayed—I must remember to pack an electric torch. As it was, arrayed in pyjamas and dressing gown, I crept down the stairs, carrying a guttering candle. Quietly I slipped the latch, and quietly I crept along the garden path to my much-needed sanctuary. How silly to worry about such an easy business I thought. And then, I heard Driver growl !

Alone amongst the inhabitants of the house and its surroundings he had heard me at my nocturnal prowlings. In a moment or two I heard his pattering along the path, and then his low growl outside the door of my refuge. It would take Lem Putt to describe my feelings properly. Suffice it to say, that more than ever was my present abode a much-needed sanctuary. It was twenty-five yards to the front door, and outside the door of the hut in which I sat was a strange dog, at least a dog who had known me only a few days. True, he was doing his rightful duty, and I knew it. But I was doing mine. Did he know that ? Would he realize its necessity, or would he be so self-centred as to consider only his side of the case ? That was the question for me, and what I suffered whilst considering it from every angle no one will ever know.

He sniffed at the door and growled again. I comforted myself with the thought that most dogs and I have ever been good friends ; and, praying that Driver would recognize my quality, I opened the door an inch or two. Then, to his shaggy countenance which showed like a blue-grey sponge in the light of my candle, I said, " Good dog, Driver."

Never have I been so relieved to see a dog wag his tail. Here and now I apologize to Driver for my previous mistrust. He is a dog of great discrimination, and he escorted me to the front door with manifest expressions of goodwill, for which I hugged him before I wished him good-night.

But this morning my ribald family have left no doubt in my mind that the joke is on me.

* * * * * *

This Cornish peace is having its effect on me, in that I am forgetting, as no farmer should, to keep my weather eye open for snags. In rural society talk is reckoned of little account, and the man who cannot prove his words by suitable action is considered by his neighbours to have been tried in the balance and found wanting. Having lived all my life under this rule I have learned by experience always to keep a guard upon my tongue, lest it should lead me either to the judgment seat or stool of repentance before my neighbours. But, as I say, this Cornish tranquillity has lulled my customary vigilance to sleep.

It was this way. Yesterday evening my wife and I wandered over to Sancreed to call on some friends, the afore-mentioned artist and his wife. Placid conversation washed down with copious draughts of cyder seemed an admirable mixture and devoid of all danger, but when another couple called to share it, I was badly caught out. Somehow or other I let out that I was in the habit of riding with my small daughter, and at this the lady's eyes gleamed with interest. She inquired whether Pam and I had brought riding clothes, and if so, whether we would like a ride on the morrow. We had brought some Jodhpurs, so what could I say, save that we should be overjoyed ? Subsequent conversation told me that she and her husband were thrust-ers to hounds ; that they had eight hunters ; and that to-morrow morning I should have the best mount Cornwall could produce. On my way home I damned Cornwall's dulling influence and my own foolish tongue, and Pam's subsequent exultation at the news did little to comfort me.

So, this morning, immediately after breakfast Pam and I set out for Sancreed. On the way I consoled myself with remembering that the wife and mother had extracted a promise from me that I would take care of her offspring, and one from both of us, that all jumping should be taboo. Our hostess met us, all smiles, and soon afterwards the three of us were mounted, and ambling up the lane towards the moor.

And soon I realized the extent of my foolishness, which would have been great enough in any district. But here ! Think of it ! A strange horse, a strange country, and stone walls no matter in what direction I looked ! I had completely forgotten that in Cornwall a ride means on the average about twenty jumps to the mile ! Another difficulty for me was that our guide was a very pretty young woman ; which meant that if she invited me to jump walls, I must, for the honour of my sex, have a go. Again I damned myself and Cornwall.

But I need not have worried. " Leave it to the mare and don't fuss her," were her instructions, and so it was. Cornish hunters may not be very fast perhaps, but aren't they clever ? They scramble on the top of a wall, pause there for a split second, and jump down. Just as easy as kissing your hand. Confidential isn't the word for our mounts' behaviour. Virtue seemed to be able to balance herself and my sixteen stone on an eighteen inch wide wall like a back-alley cat ; and Jorrocks cared for Pam like a doting father. For your cleverness, your courtesy, and for restoring to me some of my lost nerve, Virtue and Jorrocks and your charming owner, I will be ever grateful, and as I tidy up this Cornish notebook I salute all three of you from far off Wilts.

With what arrogance did Pam and I return to an anxious wife and mother, who, when she heard the tale of our escapade, contented herself by remarking, " I always knew you were a fool." Which, of course, is true enough, but here let me record that this fool " rejoiced in his folly."

       *   *   *   *   *   *

I have long admired some of our elder statesmen for their daring in using the aeroplane as a means of transport. Men who have not flown until late middle-age seem to think nothing of flying here, there, and everywhere, when their new job demands such swift travel. In fact I have one friend, who, though so badly crippled with rheumatism that he can hardly walk, sometimes on the same day has his breakfast in Vienna and his dinner in London. It beats me. If an unkind fate should ever lift me to a high place in the councils of the nation—which Heaven forfend—I am certain that I should soon get the sack for refusing to fly.

Naturally I have been jeered at for this cowardice by some of my air-minded friends, and assured by others that I should enjoy a trip in a plane ; but, until a week ago, I took no notice of either. I had no need to fly, and while that state of things obtained, the land was good enough for me.

But the other day a young gentleman about a year old shamed me properly. He stood on some short straw in a Cornish cow-house, and chewed the cud placidly while his owner related his exploit. He was a little pedigree Jersey bull, who at ten days old had come over in an aeroplane from his birthplace in the Channel Islands. His present owner's landlord, wishing to reward his tenant for winning

Bull Calf

a clean milk competition, had sent him a pedigree bull calf by this means. Well, I give my bovine aeronaut best, but I shall try not to emulate him until I'm, what we call in Wilts, " force put."

His present owner took me round his farm, and showed me that farming in Cornwall is no easy method of getting a living, however pleasant and easy-going it may appear at first glance. Many of his little fields sloped at an angle of forty-five, and his life must be one continuous battle with bracken and stones. But his stock was of the finest, and all his farming was well done. It occurs to me that the more difficult the conditions the better is the farming—not because of any special virtue in the farmer, but because he is very definitely, " force put."

*   *   *   *   *   *

Harvest in this district is a good three weeks later than in my native county, and just now it is in full swing. The minute corn fields show up so bravely amidst the pastures that town visitors are apt to think that a lot of corn is grown ; but the main business of Cornish farming is dairy-ing, vegetables, and pigs. From what I can find out from the farmers I have been privileged to meet, very few Cornish farmers voted against the Milk Marketing Board, and there is no doubt that this institution has brought money to the dairying industry in Far West England. One man defended this rather well, I thought.

" Years ago," he said to me, " we produced the richest milk in England, and got the lowest price. Now we get about the same as those who produce comparatively much poorer milk. What's wrong with that ?"

I will admit that I, a Wiltshire dairy farmer, could find no adequate answer. I daresay there is one, for Wiltshire has suffered by the new method of milk marketing in about the same proportion as Cornwall has gained ; but after a week or so's good living on Cornish cream and butter made from Guernsey milk I felt too full and too content to argue further.

But Cornwall is full of surprises. Just north of Penzance there is, I was told, some agricultural land, which is worth more money in pounds sterling to till than to use for building. One especially valuable bit of this is known as the golden acre. Well, it's nice to find that the plough can beat the brick even in one acre ; and while that state of things obtains there is still hope for England, or at any rate for Cornwall.

*   *   *   *   *   *

This morning I drove down to Newlyn to watch the trawlers unload their catch. If any farmer wants to cheer himself by watching some of his fellows earning their living in a much harder calling than his own, he cannot do better than to watch fisherman at work.

Their mode of life cannot be any more profitable than farming ; their work is obviously more risky ; while of comfort during its performance, either in or out of harbour, there is none. Besides, even in the matter of scent, dung is much pleasanter stuff to handle at any stage of its career than fish can ever be. True, to watch the Newlyn fishermen unloading their catch on a fine summer morning was pleasant enough ; but even to imagine either the unloading or the catching of the fish in bad weather made me vow never in future to permit anyone to grouse about the price of fish in my hearing without making a protest.

This morning the Newlyn fishermen had a fine catch of pilchards, in some cases so heavy that valuable nets had been lost or damaged. They told me that Italy has always been their best customer for these fish, and they seemed worried lest this country's African aspirations should make them lose this market. It seemed strange to find repercussions of international affairs in such a lovely little fishing village.

*   *   *   *   *   *

But Cornwall is not all farming and fishing and bathing, even when on holiday. I have always looked upon it as the headquarters of painting ; but this last ten days have shown me that in this county the theatre is very much alive. Thanks to Cornwall and some brave spirits who appreciate her quality and that of some writers long since dead, I have been privileged to see some of their works performed in ideal settings.

When a boy of about thirteen I was taken firmly to London for an intensive week of Shakespeare, and until this holiday I had not renewed my acquaintance with him, save through the medium of print.   How much luckier are Pam and hosts of other children who have been able to watch several of his and other writers' masterpieces, played in admirable fashion in a natural theatre. They have seen Malvolio strut before granite cliffs ; Oberon and Puck flit between tree trunks as their creator intended ; Shylock sharpen his knife before a backcloth of sea and sky ; and the Jackdaw of Rheims flutter on the edge of a precipice.

In these days of all-conquering films, plays of any kind are hard to come by in the provinces, so to those who are too old or too timid to bathe or boat or fish I can recommend a Cornish holiday, in that it will enable them to meet a host of old friends playing their several parts in the open air. Indeed, now that this Shakespeare Festival is established I cannot see Cornish folk letting it die for want of support. Why even the pixies would have something to say to such treachery, and what Cornish man or woman dare risk their displeasure ?

* * * * * *

Everything must have an ending, even a holiday, and to-morrow we are off back to Wiltshire and work. For a whole fortnight I have done nothing, save a little lazy bathing. For fourteen days I have been the accredited representative of the famous Messrs. Doolittle and Dally ; I have done little and dallied much. Lovely !

At first I could not make out why I was so completely happy in my sloth. True, a general feeling of " There's always to-morrow " seemed to rule everywhere. Was this, I wondered, a legacy from the Spaniards who came to Cornwall many years ago ? Did they marry the Cornish lassies, and so transmit Manana to succeeding generations ? Or was this absence of hurry amongst modern Cornish folk the result of the mild, moist climate ?

But I was too content to worry overmuch about this problem, and it was not until yesterday morning that I discovered the secret of Cornwall's gracious charm. Just after breakfast, when I was in the middle of my first pipe, our hostess asked me what I was going to do that day. I replied to the effect that I did not know, that I did not care, and that somehow or other in Cornwall I never did want to do anything, but that I was very happy so to be. To which blissful remark she replied, " An' why should 'ee want to do anythin' ? Lor bless 'ee, there's no hurry west o' Plymouth." And, take it from me, there just isn't, thanks be.

So now, good-bye Cornwall, and many thanks to you and

your peace for an ideal holiday. In the future, when the mechanical bustle of my Wiltshire farm becomes too much for me, or when business forces me to be sucked into that hideous maelstrom which is London, I shall comfort myself by thinking of your peaceful, colourful countryside, or rather that " There's no hurry west o' Plymouth."

      *   *   *   *   *   *

Feeding calves

Back to Work

The generally accepted idea concerning holidays is that one returns home rested and refreshed in both mind and body, and eager to tear into stacks of work. With me things do not seem to work in that fashion. Somehow or other I cannot shake off the lethargy acquired in Cornwall ; and the seemingly boundless energy of my Wiltshire friends and neighbours makes me feel very tired.

But, luckily for me, circumstances do not permit me to give way to my natural sloth. Having had my holiday, my men must needs have theirs. Indeed, I am convinced that holidays are more necessary for employees than for employers. No matter what the business may be, the man who owns and manages it, while he will usually work harder and for longer hours than his employees, will always contrive to obtain a considerable amount of fun and interest out of his toil. But to do the same job for a wage, day after day, week in week out throughout the year, must surely become very monotonous after a while. It is one thing to milk one's own cows, but very definitely another to do the same for other people's.

So, already Charlie, the head dairyman, has disappeared, and the others will take a week in rotation. More than that we cannot manage, for when one's farming staff is a small one, the absence of one pair of hands makes a big difference. But golly ! I hope Charlie won't return in the same bone lazy state of mind as his employer.

*   *   *   *   *   *

Another thing which has made me feel that life in

Wiltshire is very real and very earnest was to find my desk piled high with accumulated correspondence. Which, I must confess, is entirely my own fault. Prior to my holiday I threatened my secretary with all sorts of pains and penalties if she forwarded anything save vital matters. Consequently, she amused herself during my holiday by writing polite notes to all and sundry to the effect that I was away from home but would deal with the matter immediately on my return. Incidentally, she is now basking by the sea, so I have been dealing with the harvest of my leisure unaided.

Bills—a fine crop, almost too heavy to be satisfactorily harvested with the modest equipment at my disposal. (Note : Holidays are nice, but devilish expensive.) Letters —as rank and plentiful as Fall keep after September rain ; with here and there a small cheque, showing shyly amidst the aftermath of my holiday like the occasional cornflower in the roadside bank. It is at times like this that one is apt to envy the days of one's grandfather, when the receipt of a letter was a comparatively rare cocurrence.

But there was a bright spot or two in this huge pile of assorted paper. Once again I found evidence, written evidence this time, that September is an unusually attractive month, in that it enables the countryman to enjoy the sports and pleasures of both summer and winter. There was an invitation to shoot partridges ; one card of otter-hunt meets and another of cubbing ; a ticket for a day's fishing ; and a lot of news concerning forthcoming gymkhanas, tennis, and cricket. Yes, I like September. But how I wish I could have another fortnight's holiday at home !

*   *   *   *   *   *

At long last the drought has broken, and we have had

enough rain to ensure some Autumn keep. For which relief
much thanks. As a result my lovely Wilts is getting
greener and more lovely daily, which pleases me greatly.
In all her gowns I admire her, but she looks better in a green
frock than in one of dull, barren brown.

And this rain has brought not only grass everywhere,
but also mushrooms ; to some farmers a saleable quantity,
and to me enough for a perfect breakfast. Did I say that I
liked September ? Well, it is a sentence which will bear
repetition ; and so will the mushrooms.

*　　*　　*　　*　　*　　*

I have just returned from doing a job of work at
Ashridge. I put it like that to save my face, but in truth I
must admit that for some time I have looked upon these
visits to the Bonar Law College as a holiday.

Still, there is much to be said for the pleasant informality
of Ashridge. One gives a lecture, and in the lecture room
one tries to answer questions satisfactorily ; but the dickens
of it is that one cannot escape from one's audience after
leaving the lecture room. Oh no ! Various eager students
of politics buttonhole you in the canteen—indeed, such is
their thirst for knowledge that some have been known to
provide the lecturer with alcoholic lubrication—and then
they get right down to business in such thorough fashion
that any weak spots in one's arguments receive searching
criticism. I have a notion that this buttonholing of lec-
turers does quite as much good as the lectures, and in some
cases considerably more.

But sometimes the questions are beyond my powers to
answer. For instance, this week-end I was asked whether
my grandson would farm in the same fashion as I do. Not
yet possessing a grandson—and really I did not think I

looked old enough to possess one—I refused to pledge an unborn Englishman's credit. Should he arrive in the full-ness of time, no doubt he will find plenty of troubles to welcome him without his grandsire manufacturing any.

*   *   *   *   *   *

The way in which people are talking about the existing plague of rabbits annoys me. The trouble is that I cannot agree with the arguments of either townsfolk or farmers ; which, of course, leaves me an Ishmael without a friend in either camp.

The townsman's argument seems to be this. " There are too many rabbits. They are doing the farmer a lot of harm. The price they fetch for meat does not pay the cost of catching. Well, why must the farmer be such a dog in the manger ? He won't catch the rabbits himself ; why not let other folk catch them ? Why not do some one else a good turn and at the same time rid himself of these des-tructive vermin ? Why not let the townsman have a bit of cheap sport ? At least, why not give the unemployed the chance of a cheap dinner ?"

Of course, all that sounds all right, and again and again I find this argument put forward in the correspondence columns of the newspapers. But farmers ignore it, and steadfastly refuse to let anyone, save employees, friends, or shooting tenants, even look at their rabbits. Result, the townsman looks upon the farmer as a niggardly, petty land baron, the reason being that he has no conception that rabbits are more welcome on any farm than is the uninvited human stranger. At the risk of being held up to execration as an inhuman brute I must give the true reason for this. Both rabbits and trespassers are damn nuisances to the

Both rabbits and trespassers are damn nuisances
to the farmer

farmer ; but, while he can kill off the former without unpleasant consequences to himself, to treat the latter in similar fashion would mean an inglorious end to his farming career at the hands of the public hangman.

The countryside is a complicated business—how many times have I written that—and all sorts of people are engaged in it. Only those who pay for their footing have any right there, and only those who pay for their footing can be kept under any sort of control. Shooting rights have a market value ; and, while the law will not permit the farmer to deprive himself of the right to kill rabbits, if he has let his shooting he is in honour bound to protect his tenant's interests. A crowd of townsfolk or unemployed chasing all over the place would soon render the sporting rights of a farm valueless, not because of the loss of the few rabbits they might catch and take away, but for two other reasons. Firstly, because their activities would disturb all the game ; and secondly, because, not having any interest in the countryside over which they sported, through ignorance they would be certain to do all kinds of damage to its farming.

Some years ago there was a proposal to build a large central school in the middle of my farm. I besought my landlord to offer a site for it at the edge of my farm instead. The argument which succeeded was this. " You wouldn't put two hundred rabbits in a burrow in the middle of my farm, would you ? In fact, if you did I have a notion that I could claim damages. Well, two hundred children in a brick and tile burrow would be ten times worse from my point of view."

And that is the farmer's argument whenever it is proposed that he should let anyone and everyone get after his unwanted rabbits, and to my mind it is a reasonable and sensible one.

——Rather bear those ills we have,

Than fly to others that we know not of ?

But instead of living up to that motto, many farmers to-day cannot bear the rabbit ills they have without whining. " It doesn't pay to catch our rabbits," they say. " There should be a tariff on imported rabbits, sufficiently high to raise rabbit prices to a remunerative level."

And here I quarrel with them flatly. If we are to have tariffs, let us have them on our crops and stock—the mellowed fields of England want no tariff help to produce vermin. Besides, were rabbits, through a tariff policy, to become a profitable side-line of our farming, we should never get rid of the vermin. Better far to use tariffs to make the production of first-class farm produce highly profitable, and then a prosperous farming industry would soon get rid of its rabbits, even if they only fetched a farthing each.

The trouble to-day is this. Two or three warm, dry seasons, warm dry winters as well as summers, have resulted in an enormous increase in the rabbit population. The warm winters enabled the rabbits to breed all the year round, and the dry winters and springs have meant a complete absence of that dread disease, liver-fluke, which usually kills off millions of rabbits every year. So the British farmer is faced with a horde of rabbits, and a very low price for them when caught.

Rabbit catching can be divided into two distinct parts—the cream and the skim milk. The cream is composed of the easily caught rabbits, those usually captured from October to January. At any price it pays to catch these—the fools of the family, so to speak—and anyone is only too pleased to have the chance to get after them. But it is the skim milk—those clever rabbits which remain alive in February and March—which must be destroyed if there is to be any appreciable reduction in the rabbit population next summer. Those rabbits which will not bolt, which dodge all snares, and which are grown old in cunning. There is no sport in their capture, but only hard unprofitable work. No townsman will do it for fun ; no unemployed man would do it for profit ; only an irate farmer will sweat for half a day with pick and shovel in order to obtain a rabbit which, more often than not, is valueless owing to the line ferret's activities.

But it is penny wise and pound foolish for any farmer to cease rabbiting as soon as the bag does not pay the expenses. His correct procedure is to skim the cream of his rabbiting during the winter months when rabbits are saleable ; and in the spring to gas the skim milk in their burrows. And of one thing I am convinced—the dearer rabbits are, the more rabbits will be found in England's countryside.

     *   *   *   *   *   *

All men have their enthusiasms. With some it is money ; with others women ; some take to drink ; others to thieving ; some become keen on some particular brand of politics or religion ; according to age and capabilities some go mad about sport, gambling, art, or free-masonry ; and a few unfortunates give way to drugs ; but every man in the world must be enthusiastic about something or another, if he is to refrain from suicide. The happy man is he whose daily work provides him with the necessary thrills, and such a man is my dealer friend who sold me Pam's pony.

Dealers, like poets, are born not made, and this man

was blessed at birth with the priceless possession of a natural flair for dealing. This he exploits to the full. Not for one waking moment during his day does he ever forget that he is a dealer. He is quite willing to be a dealer in anything, with anybody, at any moment. He has a useful small-holding, and since I have known him it has been his habit to rise early and work late. Presumably he sleeps soundly, but sometimes I have conjured up pictures of him doing one deal with his Maker during sleep about the lowest rent to a good tenant for a comfortable place in Heaven, and another with the devil concerning the lowest cash price for his sultry domain. It seems inconceivable to me that he would fail to make these bargains satisfactorily, or that he would be unable to sublet the former to the devil at a higher rent, and resell the latter to some ribbon builder at a handsome profit. Anyway, as far as my knowledge goes, he never misses an opportunity to do a deal.

He gave me a taste of his quality early this morning. Pam and I set off in the dark to go cubbing. The hounds were meeting at my dealer friend's village, and, as we were nearing this I caught sight of him wandering about in one of his pastures. A hail brought him to the fence, but when I asked him if he were going cubbing, he shook his head.

"Naw. Ye see, I be main busy. Thease yer musheroons do vetch a smart vew aypence. I zilled thirty shillin's-wuth las' wik."

Then he caught sight of Pam's pony.

"My, but don't thic pony look well. You know, I zilled 'ee too cheap. But Miss Street 'ave growed out of 'im. Thee't ha' to git her a nice cob, 'bout fourteen 'ands."

"Time enough for that," I answered, "Toby'll do her

business all right this season. Well, we must jog on or we shall be late. Sorry you can't make it."

And away we went, leaving him to his mushrooms.

As we jogged I remarked to Pam that her friend was right about Toby being too small for her, and that if her legs continued to grow at last summer's rate her feet would touch the ground next spring. A few minutes afterwards we were in the thick of it—dodging along dew-drenched narrow rides through small coppices ; getting in the way and out of the way of Master, huntsman, and whips ; sometimes galloping for dear life ; at others trying to keep fidgety mounts still ; and enjoying ourselves thoroughly.

Then, all of a sudden, during a short run between two small covers, I caught sight of our dealer friend on a cob of about fourteen hands. The whole business was handled perfectly. He stayed out about twenty minutes, during which time he managed to jump a hurdle, to scramble up and down a steep bank, to exhibit a cob which would stand still or go as required. And every blooming thing he made that cob do was performed where Pam and I could not fail to notice it. Having thus sown the good seed, he departed to his more or less lawful avocations.

I was relating this to a neighbour this evening, and he told me a tale concerning our dealer friend which illustrates still more clearly that with him dealing comes first, last, and all the time. My neighbour had given him a lift to a sale, and when they were approaching a main road, which ran at right angles to the lane on which they were travelling the dealer sang out, " Hey ! Lookeezee ! There's a 'oss running away."

Down the hill towards the cross-roads a horse was trailing the forecarriage of a van behind him, and chasing the runaway were two men in a car. An A.A. scout stopped the horse at the cross-roads, and when my two friends arrived, its owner was busy unharnessing it from the wreck. Immediately the dealer said to my neighbour, " Let I out, zur. Let I out. I bought a 'oss cheap once, jist atter 'ee'd runned away."

My friend did so, and subsequently walked near enough to the horse to overhear the conversation.

" H'm ! " said the dealer, eyeing the horse critically. " 'Ad a runaway, I see."

" Yes ! " said the owner of the horse.

" Hump ! Pity, fer 'ee'm a nice enough 'oss. Don't want to zell un I spose ? "

" No ! " said the man shortly.

" H'm ! I zee. Once they've runned away they be most times allus liable. But I be used to sich 'osses. 'Tis onsafe to trust 'em on the road again nowadays wi' all this yer moty traffic. But I could vind 'ee a job on the land. Sure you don't want to zell un ? "

" I've told you I don't," replied the owner. " He's all right, and 'tisn't his fault that he bolted. Fool of a boy took his bridle off, that's all."

" H'm ! " said the dealer. " That do scare 'em fer sure. I knows 'ow 'tis wi' boys nowadays. Too much dratted schoolin', an' too little stick. I'd gi'e 'ee a goodish price fer un, zno ?"

" Not to-day you won't," said the man, " and I'd have you know I'm busy."

There was no mistaking the annoyance in that final remark. After all, any man whose horse has just run away is naturally in no mood to be trifled with, so the dealer was now forced to abandon the role of possible purchaser.

" Oh ! " he said to the owner of the horse. " Oh ! I see. H'm ! Anybody hurt ? "

But this aspect of the runaway was not considered even until all the chance of a deal was over.

               *   *   *   *   *   *

Modern youth's love of noise puzzles me. Yesterday afternoon I was watching two girls and two lads, all about twenty years old, playing a good fast game of tennis on a hard court. The tennis was so good that they could not have been thinking about or listening to anything but their game ; and yet they had a five valve portable wireless set blaring to high heaven the while.

We older folk who were watching the play all decided that we could do without this noise, so I switched it off. Not until the set was over and the players were talking together and to us whilst fixing up another set did any of them notice that the wireless was silent. But when they did ! " Oh ! Someone's switched off the wireless," they cried, and all four ran to switch it on. This done they returned to play fast tennis.

Then, being a crabbed old man, I switched it off again.

               *   *   *   *   *   *

Whew ! How it rains ! The later districts will suffer in consequence, I'm afraid, but hereabouts in the south practically all the harvest is safely gathered in.

But even in my own county there are some fields still in stook, and this warm wet is making the grain grow out. In most cases it is late spring corn after sheep which is still out, but here and there one is hard put to it to find any reason for uncleared fields after such a fine August. A friend of mine told me only yesterday of a farmer who groused about the rain, and who, when my friend got down

The fact remains milk is largely Water

to cases with him, admitted that he had only fifteen acres of corn all told ! If it kept fine until Christmas he would still have some harvesting to do, I should imagine.

One thing the rain has done, it has raised the milk yield. It is rather ticklish to talk of water in connection with milk, but the fact remains that all milk is largely water, and that in a dry time the yield goes down. One may have the most elaborate water supply, and a generous number of troughs, but in drought cattle cannot graze in comfort. True, in dry weather if they get an ample supply of drinking water they will thrive excellently, but they won't put it in the pail. I do not think it is the lack of grass which lowers the yield, but that dry grass is unpalatable. Consequently, during a drought it is well to change a dairy herd's pasture frequently.

*   *   *   *   *   *

Sometimes I doubt whether the powers that be will ever succeed in making English people internationally-minded, especially countryfolk. In spite of all there has been in the papers lately concerning them, how many of us—by us I mean the ordinary mythical men and women in the street or on the farm—know exactly what " sanctions " are or should be ? I, for one, must plead guilty to, if not complete ignorance, only a very vague idea ; and I daresay that I have plenty of company.

In spite of the fact that modern transport is supposed to have made our frontier, the Rhine, what would be the first reaction of the average English person to the news that several hundred people had been killed by flood, earthquake, or other disaster in, say, China, or Czechoslovakia ? It sounds awful, I admit, but in many cases it would be, " Oh Chinese ! " or what is worse, " Serve 'em right, for being

Czechoslovakians. I say, how did the Arsenal get on to-day ? ''

I do not suggest that either remark is a thing about which to brag, but I do suggest that either would be made in many instances. And of one thing I am convinced—when the time is ripe for English people to abandon their insular attitude to international matters they will do so of their own accord, and until then orders from well-meaning reformers to that effect will have a hindering rather than a helping influence.

* * * * * *

Land I think, is coming into its own again, both as an investment and for farming. To-day it is becoming rapidly more and more difficult to find a farm which is really desirable, and those of this quality which do come into the market, either for sale or to rent, change hands quietly without ever appearing in the advertisement columns of the newspapers.

This does not mean that there is a fortune to be made at farming, but it does mean that the chances are a trifle better than they have been in recent years. Possibly one reason for this is that the long period of bad times has squeezed out those unfortunate farmers who were unable to stand the financial strain ; and that at long last the bulk of the war-time inflation of values has been written off. In consequence, the young farmer who begins his business career at to-day's values for stock and implements, if he knows his job and works hard, has a chance to make a modest living at to-day's prices for his produce.

* * * * * *

Two mornings this week my small daughter has awakened me at 4.30. With many groans the fond father heaved himself out of bed, shaved, breakfasted, and rode off in the pitch dark with his offspring to go cubbing. But when, an hour or two later, the sun was up and the September morning was all lush and golden around him he gave thanks that he had conquered his natural sloth.

One may or may not help to catch a fox ; one may bucket up and down amidst rhododendrons and hazel for hours to apparently no useful purpose ; one may be tired, sleep all day afterwards, and be excruciatingly stiff next morning as a result ; but on the other side of the balance sheet of cubbing there is a long list of credit entries.

Here are a few. The certain knowledge that one's health has benefited ; the friendly company of one's neighbours of all classes—here commend me to one of my small-holder friends who rode furiously in slacks and gum boots ; the sight and sound and feel of a sunny September morning in those early hours when so few have any acquaintance with it—wet sloshy green pastures, cobwebs on the grass, squelchy woodland rides, a landscape drenched with sun and dew, the melodious accompaniment of horn and hound ; and, in my case, the continuous sight just under a bowler hat of the ecstatic grin of one very happy little girl. Definitely the balance is on the right side.

* * * * * *

How true it is that none of one's doings in the country-side can be hidden from one's neighbours ! A young friend of mine who has just taken a farm wisely decided to let the farmhouse and to live in a cottage. When his furniture arrived it was discovered that the beds would not go through the door, and so they had to be manhandled with some difficulty through an upstair window. And, according to his account and much to his annoyance, during the operation every body in the village walked slowly past the cottage and in a very few moments returned in their tracks !

I comforted him by informing him that the searchlight of public opinion is turned more strongly on the newcomer to a farm than on any other person in the land ; that by comparison, a king or a cabinet minister enjoys a cloistered privacy ; and that this state of things is all for the good of farming, which necessitates that a man shall be judged solely by his deeds.

*   *   *   *   *   *

Once again the sugar beet harvest has come round. My acreage is a small one, but the crop is good. But how I wish the sugar beet grew more like a mangold, and so could be lifted with ease !

So small is my field that we are doing the job by means of hand and prong. I am well aware that this is a slow and expensive method ; that there are all sorts of lifters on the market ; that a fair job can be done by means of a single plough with the mouldboard removed ; and also that I should know better than to lift mine as I am doing.

But I don't like sugar beet ; neither my men nor I like the messy business which results from the use of a plough ; and, although I know that I am doing wrong, I'm going to do it. After all, if a man pays the bills for the privilege of running a farm—and it is a privilege to have the ordering of some of the acres of one's native land—he should be allowed to make a few mistakes which please him.

But isn't it queer that everything in this world has a snag to it ? Nuts have shells, blackberries have thorns, plums have stones—the catalogue is endless—and, to repeat, why the dickens don't sugar beet grow like mangolds ?

In their present form only a qualified dentist could deal with them satisfactorily.

*   *   *   *   *   *

Once again I have been reminded that I am no longer my own master.   Our local ploughing match was held this week, and from the standpoints of both farmer and author I should surely have attended it.   But a job of work in London forced me to forego this useful pleasure.   However, I had a yarn this evening with a neighbour who was present, and during our chat he criticized from a new angle the modern practice here and there of mechanized cereal growing without livestock.

" When that comes to a village," he said, " in two years' time the population of that village has changed.   In these days the strength of a nation lies in the proportion of its population which stays put."

An old-fashioned argument many will say, but the more I think about it the more I become convinced that my friend was right.   We peripatetic folk see so much, but are very apt to understand so little.

And here is a verse which I came across in Mr. W. J. Blyton's recent book, " Country Airs," and which, I think our agricultural legislators would do well to learn.

> Leisurely flocks and herds,
> Cool-eyed cattle that come
> Mildly to wonted words,
> Swine that in orchards roam—
> A man and his beasts make a man
>   and his home.

By comparison with livestock farming mechanized cereal growing is merely a few children playing with a meccano set.

*   *   *   *   *   *

a Man and his beasts make a man and his home

I cannot vouch for the truth of this tale, but it is so unbelievable that it must be true. Some bright young townsfolk settled in a village, and at week-ends were in the habit of filling their house with a party of still brighter young townsfolk. Cocktails and other jollifications therefore did not finish until well on into Sunday mornings. Consequently, between ten and eleven a.m. on Sundays the household was, or wished to be, sound asleep.

Unfortunately the church was next door, and the sound of the bells woke them up ; and my informant told me that they were so lacking in taste as to ask the parson whether this disturbing noise could not be stopped on their behalf !

As an example of how not to behave in the country this is hard to beat ; but here is something even more astounding. The people in the village who were most annoyed with the newcomers' request that the church bells should not ring on Sunday mornings were the villagers who never, never, never, went to church ! ! !

*   *   *   *   *   *

Contrary to popular belief foxes seem to be on the increase. I was shooting on a Wiltshire farm the other day, and abutting on the main Exeter road from Salisbury was a patch of marrow stemmed kale of about five acres. Cover being scarce we walked the stubbles trying to drive some partridges into this, but for some reason or other the birds would not settle there.

However, we walked the kale carefully and slowly—a wet pleasure, yes very wet—and the five head we disturbed were all foxes, who trotted slowly away over the stubble towards the downs in delightfully lazy fashion.

*   *   *   *   *   *

One of my correspondents has taken me to task for never, or very rarely, mentioning women in country matters. This, I grant, is a serious omission, which I now hasten to rectify. At charades or any guessing game I am the world's prize idiot, and often at village functions I am amazed at the cleverness of most of the company. Accordingly, I was not a whit surprized to find myself winning the booby prize in a competition concerning book titles at a meeting of a local Women's Institute. Each person wore some device which was supposed to represent the title of a well-known book. I did guess one, the Rosary ; but most of my companions had a total of nearly two dozen.

But it was the quiet lady in the corner who defeated everybody, not only with her score but with a title which no one guessed. Pinned to her blouse was a card on which was printed PHARAOH. MUSSOLINI. When pressed to tell the secret she said demurely, " Hymns, Ancient and Modern."

And, as the Americans put it, we had to hand it to her.

*   *   *   *   *   *

When is a road not a road ? I ask this riddle because more and more am I becoming convinced that the problem of road traffic in this country will never be solved unless we provide a clear answer to it. What I am driving at is this— a road is not merely a track for the passage of wheeled traffic, it is a public highway, and the sooner we realize this the sooner we shall stop this horrible slaughter and endless recrimination between all classes of road users.

When is a road not a road ? When it passes through a town or a village. Let me try to illustrate.

Mr. Bill Smith lives in London, and possesses a motor car. For some perfectly legitimate reason he wishes to drive from London to Exeter. He is a good and careful driver ; he has paid for his car licence and his driving licence ; and he has insured his car against all eventualities. Having paid the bill he wants to use the road from London to Exeter as a road.

Well, why shouldn't he ? To him that road is merely a track, a speed track wherever possible. It is absurd to talk to him of the traffic speed of his ancestor's vehicles. He wishes to make use of the vehicle which modern science and invention have provided for his use. What is the good, he says, of buying a car which will do eighty miles per hour, if he cannot drive it at that speed ? He is not interested in any of the towns and villages en route ; he is not acquainted with any of their inhabitants ; but his best girl lives in Exeter, and he wants to drive down and kiss her. Surely a reasonable laudable desire ?

But here is the snag. In the village of Sedgebury Wallop, say, there live some people who have never heard of Bill Smith or of his girl ; people who perhaps have rarely visited London, and who have never visited Exeter. To them that portion of the road between those two towns which passes through Sedgebury Wallop is not a road at all. It is part of their village, their children's playground, indeed almost as much their dwelling place as the interior of their cottages. Why, they say, should Bill Smith hurtle through this portion of their village, making it possibly a death trap, and certainly a continual worry and danger in their daily lives ?

Farmer Giles' cows and his forefather's cows have ambled slowly and awkwardly along the road through the village from time immemorial. To Farmer Giles that piece of the London-Exeter road is—when his cows are walking from the farm-buildings to the meadows—a part of his farm. Without the right to use it in this fashion his farm could not be carried on.

Here Bill Smith chips into the discussion in a great hurry. " That's just it," he snorts. " Cows ! They ought not to be allowed." This sounds as though he means that cows should be exterminated. Not at all—what he really means is that considering what he is forced to pay in taxation for permission to drive a car he should be provided with a road which is clear of cows.

And here most farmers will agree with him, for most farmers are motorists ; but here most farmers will point out, and quite rightly, that the cow was on this particular road long before motors were invented, and cyclists, pedestrians, and other road users will use the same argument.

But farmers are always grumbling. Let us get back to the simple desires of the inhabitants of Sedgebury Wallop. Old Granny Bundy is crippled with rheumatism, so much

Without the right to use it in this manner
his farm could not be carried on

so that she can only toddle very slowly with the help of two sticks. On the other side of the village street from her cottage her son is lying dangerously ill. Surely she has enough worries, poor old soul, without being terrified whenever she crosses the road to visit him? Again, to-day cottage mothers spend their days in fear for what may be happening to little Tommy or Maud on their way to and from school. Is this condition of things a sign of progress or of what?

And that seems to me to be our road problem to-day? The motorist considers that he is paying enough to be allowed to use his car according to its capabilities; but when he isn't motoring he looks upon the road as a public highway for all classes of users.

It would seem therefore that the solution must lie in the provision of two definite classes of roads, rather than in speed limits and signs and traffic lights and bad feeling between all classes of road users. Our ancestors had too much sense to put the railway train upon the ordinary roads; they built a special track for it. For through traffic we shall have to build special roads. Roads with a partition down their middles, each half three vehicles wide, so that it will be impossible for any vehicles to meet on them, and wide enough that speed need have no limit.

Then, at suitable intervals we must provide egress from these speed tracks to our existing network of public highways, on which the maximum speed shall be no higher than twenty miles per hour, and possibly only half that figure. This would give us public speed tracks and public highways, two badly needed things, for to-day we have neither.

Granted, the cost would be heavy, but considering two things—the present daily slaughter and injury on our existing road system and the number of our unemployed people—the argument that it would be money well spent is difficult to refute.

Under such conditions Bill Smith would be able to get to his girl in Exeter at least an hour quicker and without endangering or annoying anybody ; and I, who perhaps want to call on a friend at Sedgebury Wallop, could drive at ninety miles per hour to within three miles of that village, and then amble gently down the existing road to my destination without frightening poor Old Granny Bundy. Also, then everybody would know the answer to my riddle, " When is a road not a road ? "

*　　　*　　　*　　　*　　　*　　　*

I have just had a book sent to me from U.S.A., which deals with the position of American livestock under the A.A.A., or to give it its full title, the Agricultural Adjustment Act. I have not read all of it, but I have read enough to make me weep for man's idiocy. The statement that the first great *achievement* was the slaughter of so many thousand pregnant sows was bad enough, but when I came to the copies of the CORN-HOG REDUCTION CONTRACT I gave up and went to bed thinking of how Almighty must be regretting the creation of man. Think of it ! A solemn legal contract between the farmer and the state, whereby the former receives state money for reducing his production!

Here surely is one thing which we do not want to copy from America. The whole purpose of a farmer's life is based on the idea of trying to be a better farmer—that is to produce more produce—each succeeding year. Take that away ; go further and pay him for producing less than he is able ; and farming ceases to be a satisfactory life for any sane man who wishes to keep his self-respect. Which means, of course, that farming ceases. Which must mean that factories will cease also, and that towns and cities will soon moulder away.

There is, I know, one school of agricultural opinion which considers reduction of production in this country as a possible solution to our farming's ills, but I, for one, hope that this will never come to pass.

*   *   *   *   *   *

What a lot of things we countryfolk can have for the taking—sometimes legitimately, and sometimes, it must be confessed, almost bordering on theft. But perhaps theft is the wrong word—the old army term, scrounging, best describes this business.

Now is the season for rural scrounging, or, if you like, the season of the poor man's harvest. Nuts, mushrooms, sloes, blackberries—all are to be had for the gathering. And from the number of people of all ages and classes whom I have seen purposefully wandering over my farm and the surrounding country recently there is no doubt that the arts of scrounging, and of making jam and sloe gin, are very much alive.

*   *   *   *   *   *

Summer has definitely said Good-bye. It rains and it blows ; but chiefly it rains. Day after day with just an occasional glimpse of the sun to cheer us up. And this we need, for in the country the weather is the warp in the loom of life. It is our livelihood, our pleasure, our friend, our enemy, and, in consequence, our continuous study.

Just now the countryside looks very damp and drear. Although the trees have not yet begun to turn colour— except for the elms, which already show lemon patches to the sky—they have lost their summer lustre. It is rather queer to see them looking so sad, and yet standing on a carpet of vivid green grass. Just as though the Clerk of the Weather had married Spring and Autumn by mistake.

A Nice Time of Year

I suppose one reason why most countryfolk like Autumn is because they know so well what must soon lie in store for them. Winter cannot be so very far away, and so every genial autumn day seems doubly precious. And when, as sometimes happens, Autumn smiles on into November, one revels in this early clipping of Winter's wings.

October especially is an enjoyable month for farmers. The perishable harvest is safely under cover ; the harvesting of roots is in full swing ; the staff of the farm is settled for another year ; ploughing and sowing for next harvest are well under way ; fairs and shows are finished for the year ; the tenancy is safe for another two years ; the town visitors have disappeared ; the plan of campaign for the next twelve months has been settled ; and there is nothing to do but to get on with it in peace and privacy. For a few weeks anyway the weather cannot hinder the farm work very much, if at all. All the men know what their work will be next day without orders ; the dairy has been made up to strength ; there is still some grass for the cows ; there can be no frost hard enough to stop the ploughs ; and so most farms are well-ordered hives of industry, which seemingly run of their own accord.

Of course, they don't. Without the eye of the man whose pocket will suffer if things go wrong, things will go wrong, be the weather ever so helpful. But still, provided the farmer gets round his farm sharp at seven every morning, he can get away for an occasional day's shooting or hunting without suffering many qualms of conscience. The partridge is now much stronger on the wing than he was in September ; while even though there is too much leaf for covert shooting, the pheasant is now in season, and it is amazing how many can be found along the hedgerows. Oh, it's a nice time of year, both for work and play.

* * * * * *

At last the weather has cheered up a trifle, and sugar beet lifting is a slightly less messy business. Just now there seems to be beet everywhere, even in this part of the world ; and I imagine that parts of the Eastern Counties are beet and nothing else.

I often wonder whether the average townsman has ever given the British farmer credit for the way in which he has adapted his farming to deal with this alien crop. It just shows that he will do anything and grow anything, provided he can see reasonable hope of a small profit by so doing. Few farmers, I think, like sugar beet as a crop, and most of them would have preferred—I know I should—that our politicians had seen fit to further our old-established branches of farming. But the pundits chose otherwise— the lure of something new was so attractive. So the British farmer shrugged his shoulders at such childishness, but proceeded immediately to get on with this new job and make it pay him. And that is the acid test of all farming and farming policy, a thing which our rulers would do well to keep in mind—the British farmer can and will do anything when it pays ; but he can't and won't do a damn thing when it doesn't pay.

* * * * * *

The other day I overtook a wagon fitted with head and tail ladders, which was piled high with bundles of yellow thatch, Nothing very remarkable in that, I grant, but in this case the wagon was shod with huge pneumatic tyres.

These things are an undoubted improvement on the iron tyre, but they do look queer. The artist who dares to paint a wagon fitted with them will be a brave man ; for underneath a wagon load of straw they look as bad as shorts on a fat woman. Still, they did provide yet one more illustration that the British farmer does use modern invention to help him whenever possible.

*　　*　　*　　*　　*　　*

More and more I am coming to the conclusion that the undoubted flair for the art of governing human beings which the English nation possesses was acquired in England's villages rather than in her towns ; although I will admit that nowadays it is the town which handles the reins. The other day I said as much to Mr. Arthur Bryant, and he told me a delightful story in support of this view.

Part of our success in governing people is, apparently, due to our non-belief in logic, for which, he told me, we are the despair of continental peoples. At some date in our history, at the time when the village constable was responsible for law and order in his village, there was a law on the statute book which provided dire pains and penalties for anyone who used bad language. At that time most country-folk swore as charmingly and continuously in their general conversation as they do now ; and so the law was a dead letter. In such circumstances a logical nation would have repealed it, but not the English. They left it on the statute book, and just ignored it. Why ?

Sometimes in a village there would be one man who was an infernal nuisance to everybody—a wife-beater, a drunkard, and a lazy good-for-nothing. And then one day he swore in the constable's hearing ; whereupon this good man said, " Ah ! Here is this most excellent law," and proceeded to put it into operation. A better example of the art of successful government I have yet to find.

I told this tale to a farmer friend of mine, who is a local J.P., and in return he told me of his initiation into public work. He was a young bachelor on his first farm, and one evening the old Parish Clerk called on him, and said, " We've elected thee Awverzeer."

My friend, having other fish to dry, answered that he was grateful for the honour but that he was not interested in public work of any kind.

" Bain't 'ee ? " replied the ancient. " Then thee't damn zoon will be. The books be comin' up to-morrer."

And so, willy-nilly, this young man was forced to take his share in the government of his friends and neighbours.

What is the result ? Here is his comment on the day's work at some Petty Sessions, which has caused me furiously to think. " We gave four decisions this afternoon," he remarked to me. " Three legal and grossly unjust, and one just decision which was grossly illegal, but I was determined to have one thing right. You see, I knew the people concerned."

Is this an argument for stipendiary magistrates or one in favour of the present system ? Somehow I incline to the latter view, for in England's country life two and two seldom make exactly four, and only the man on the spot can know how to calculate them correctly. In other words, in the interests of justice it is often necessary to temper the wind to the shorn lamb, and so the spirit of the law must be invoked in addition to the letter.

* * * * * *

I 'low times be better but I bain't better off.

I was talking with a farm labourer the other day, the type of man who prior to the war earned about fifteen shillings weekly plus his house, and who is now earning forty shillings weekly with the same cottage rent free in addition. " I 'low times be better," he said, " but I bain't no better off."

When I asked him to explain he said, " Well, ye zee, 'tis this way. I don't git no more beer neet no more baccer, than I did 'fore the war, but my Missus and kids, they be a deal better off."

And tha'ts the way of it in a good many cases, I suppose —a world made by men for women. Modern transport coupled with higher prices has altered the women's life considerably, but the older farm labourer carries on in much the same fashion. Very certainly, when one sees the seething crowd of young men, women, and children in the country market towns every Saturday night, it is difficult to think that times are not considerably better. To the statement that man cannot live by bread alone, one must now add that in England's countryside neither man, woman, nor child can live without petrol. But I do think that the older breadwinners who stay at home should share in the present prosperity.

* * * * * *

I have just come across a rural story which illustrates that the true countryman soon estimates newcomers to his districts at their proper value, and one which political candidates in country constituencies should heed. Some rather famous folk in the theatre and film world took a Wiltshire country cottage for week-ends, and on Saturday nights made the village pub their headquarters. Most of the villagers who used that pub were highly delighted at being able to spend Saturday evenings in such celebrated company, but a small-holder friend of mine gave up going to the village inn soon after the newcomers arrived. A friend tried to persuade him to come down one Saturday evening, and, as an inducement, said " Ye see, the So-and-so's 'ull be down there. They be right friendly."

" Ay," retorted the small-holder, " Too friendly. Why don't 'em keep their place ? "

" That be their business," said his friend, " but they be good fun. Thee take an' come down to-night."

" Naw," said my friend. " Naw. I couldn' do that. Ye see, I got a name to keep up in these parts."

And, he meant it.

* * * * * *

Admitting the truth of the words, " God made the

country, but man made the town," the continuous spawning
and spewing of red brick all over England during recent
years has often made me wonder just how much longer
there would be any of God's handiwork remaining. I hated
every new house and bungalow which appeared as a blot
on the landscape ; I mourned the consequent lack of privacy
in rural districts ; but, like most countrymen, while I
groused, I contented myself by thinking that at any rate
there would be enough unspoilt countryside to last my
time.

I am therefore greatly indebted to Professor Stapledon
for the detailed information concerning this subject which
I found in his book, "The Land, To-day and To-morrow " ;
for this made me realize that the countryside was shrinking
with alarming rapidity. Briefly the position is this. For
the past fifteen years or so the town has robbed the countryside of over thirty thousand acres per annum. At this rate
our grandchildren will see the finish of farming in Surrey, a
London stretching to Cambridge, Salisbury and Brighton,
the urbanization of the whole of the South of England, and
a similar state of things over a wide district near every large
town throughout the country.

It seems obvious that this town encroachment will tend
to get larger rather than smaller in the immediate future.
More houses, more elbow room around them, wider roads,
more playing fields, more aerodromes, more golf courses,
and many other town requirements will have to be met.
So it seems that perhaps I myself will see the end of the
countryside in Southern England before my grandchildren
are born.

Possibly some readers may say, " Well, what of it ?   We
can neither help nor hinder modern progress.   To do that

is the Government's job." Maybe the last sentence is true enough, but the first two are not. It is everyone's business to think a little about this matter, for what is happening affects everyone's life, little or much.

The loss to farming areas may perhaps not matter. Doubtless in a few years' time we shall be able to get our food by air from Timbuctoo, and the finish of home farming will cause no inconvenience, for the nation will be content to use the remaining countryside for recreational purposes. As a farmer I should regret this, but as an Englishman I can well imagine that I should be in the minority.

But the English countryside has another value to the nation in addition to its farming possibilities. It is a very precious and very lovely possession which I imagine few people want to see disappear. Its untidy yet tidy charm, its seemingly haphazard planning, its somehow attractive inefficiency perhaps, together with its unique quality which no other nation's countryside can approach—all these things must be greater value to English people than the money value of its farming output. Surely then, we must try to find a way to save a sufficiency of it for our descendants ?

Housing, of course, is the chief problem, and it is a mistaken idea to think that the present housing shortage is merely the result of an almost complete cessation of building during the war. There has been a shortage of houses in England since 1872, and we have not yet caught up with it, in spite of the building activities of the last fifteen years. Anyone who does not believe me should drive a woman out into the country, and notice her reactions to what she sees en route. Choose one who is over sixty ; one who has never had very much money at her disposal, and one who has lived all her life in a house rented at less than a pound a week. Such a companion will be more interested in every new house or row of new houses which she sees than in any beautiful scenery you can show her. Why? Simply because she has lived all her life in company with that fear of being turned out of her house and not being able to find another.

It is useless, silly, and unkind for people who have been more favoured of fortune to ignore her side of the housing question, and to grouse continuously against the building of every new house. Women want houses—they always have wanted them, for I daresay prehistoric woman wanted a cave—and women must have houses; but remember, that in most cases it is the men who pay for them. And men nowadays most of them, work in towns, but want to live in the country. So, with the aid of modern transport the suburbs creep steadily further and further out, and the countryside which town workers seek is not there six months after their new houses are built. Still, what of it, they have got a little bit of garden to play with, and the 8.15 takes them up to work every morning, while the 6.15 fetches them home. With daylight saving, swift transport, and shorter hours they manage to obtain the best of two possible worlds.

But do they? Don't they come home tired and in no mental or physical condition to be a little ray of sunshine in the home? Or, supposing they are blest with strength to stand the strain of travelling, does being anxious all day to get home to put in a row of peas have a good effect on their work? Again, in a suburb they can have neither civic nor village pride, being merely inhabitants of a town dormitory. Aren't they almost falling between two stools?

And yet, I, a crabbed countryman who hates to see a

green field covered by red brick, realize that the countryside can no longer be the prerogative of the few ; that the most hideous bungalow on the most beautiful down is a sign of a desire for something better than a house in a town street ; and that for this reason it should not be scorned without due consideration.

What then is the solution ? A solution must be found, for both the few remaining countryfolk and the increasing number of townsfolk want to see some countryside remaining. I confess that I have no solution, but here are a few ideas for consideration, again ideas put into my head by Professor Stapledon. Has not the time come to cry " Halt " to this indiscriminate building ? To re-institute the city wall, and say, " Within these limits you may build, either up or down, but outside you shall not build ". In other words, that when a town has reached its limit, there must be a new town started, not excrescences allowed to appear ? Has not the time come to lengthen the hours of work per day, and shorten the number of days per week ? It takes time both to start or to stop either a shop, an office, or a factory. Why not keep it running for a longer continuous period when it is started ? Why not do four good days work of ten hours each, during which our interest shall be our work, and not what we are going to do after knock-off time ; and then spend three clear days in a National Park bungalow in Wales or Cumberland ? The expense ? Transport will get cheaper and quicker, and surely the future should give us more luxuries, not less. Granted, most of this is only a dream of what the future might be, but is it not towards such an ideal that we should be planning, and not towards an England which is one continuous built-up area ?

Here let me quote Professor Stapledon with regard to

the expense of such planning, which would have to be paid for by our children in the form of a sinking fund.

" If the choice was with posterity, and the decision lay between a well-arranged England with still a large acreage of farm lands and a considerable sinking fund still to be paid off, or no sinking fund and *no England*, there can be hardly a doubt as to which posterity would choose."

Remember, there is only so much land in England, and man, no matter how clever he becomes, can make no more. He can make towns, so in their making let him try to avoid as far as lies in his power the destruction and spoiling of the lovely countryside which God has given him.

    *   *   *   *   *   *

I have been thinking this evening that I have not done my duty to Professor Stapledon, in that I have not mentioned the farming side of his book, which is not only important but very interesting. Generally, people who write about the land of England are more concerned with people than with the land. I have read dozens of such books. One pleads for more prosperity for farmers ; another for higher wages for farm labourers ; some authors want to hunt or shoot over the land ; others want to enable anyone and everyone dressed in shorts to run about over it ; and very occasionally one reads a book which points out that the owner of the land is not getting exactly fat out of it.

But Professor Stapledon pleads for the well-being of the land itself. His theme, indeed his passionate theme, is that this is more important than what the land grows or than the joys or sorrows of those who own it, farm it, work on it, or pleasure on it. And yet, throughout he gives these lesser claims their rightful due. In fact, there is no aspect of the land problem with which he does not deal. Indeed,

so comprehensive is his book that after the first reading I
felt very like a staunch conservative friend of mine, who,
after reading his newspaper the other day, said, " When I
read what the National Government had done I was horri-
fied, and when I read what they proposed to do I was bloody
well terrified." For in 315 pages of print Professor Stapledon
has planned every blooming thing in our countryside.
Nothing is left to chance, nothing ; at first sight a rather
terrifying prospect.

But a second reading dispels this terror. It shows that
the author realizes the value of the land of Britain ;
that his one concern is to use it for the best advantage
of every Briton ; and I must confess that I find little
wrong with his ideas of farming policy. He deplores the
policy of subsidizing either producers or their produce.
Instead he would subsidize the land. When he suggests
that in certain cases a subsidy on a two year bare fallow,
well and truly performed, would be better business for the
nation than a subsidy on any crop, it is difficult to imagine
that any true countryman will disagree with him. Briefly
his policy is this—don't give the farmer any State money,
but let the State help him to farm better. Supply him
with manures, better quality seeds, cheap loans for land
improvement and reclamation, in fact with anything and
everything which will improve the condition of our land,
that valuable heritage which we hold in trust for posterity.

Any farmer who reads this book will heave a sigh of
relief that its author has pointed out, not only the para-
mount importance of grass in British farming, but what is
far more important, that all grasslands can be improved,
and that to obtain good arable you must first get good grass.
He will also agree that a decrease of permanent pasture and

a corresponding increase of temporary pasture is to be desired ; and that only by a system of arable-grass-stock farming can our farming industry achieve that flexibility which should be the nation's first aim in agricultural policy. Most farmers, too, will agree with Professor Stapledon's policy of owner-occupiers in preference to land nationalization ; and that the land community cannot have it both ways—there must be either nationalization or drastic State powers to ensure that the land is used to the best advantage.

One criticism which occurs to me is that for such a book to effect any material change in agricultural policy it must be read by the average townsman, and, more important still, by the average townswoman ; who, generally speaking, prefer such strong medicine in much smaller doses and in more easily digested form. Such phrases as " the co-efficient of rural-icity "—a word, by the way, which does not seem to be in the Oxford dictionary—take some swallowing.

* * * * * *

More and more I notice being put forward the plea for more and better roads, and for cheaper transport of all kinds in order to provide easier access to the beauties of our countryside for our enormous town population. So here, at the risk of being thought selfish, I would suggest that if we are to preserve our beauty spots as beauty spots the time has come to make them more difficult to reach rather than more easy. This is an age of crowds and too often a crowd destroys natural beauty by the mere fact of finding it. Instead of more roads to beauty spots I should like to see all roads destroyed within three miles of all beauty spots, in order to ensure that only those who appreciate them sufficiently to walk that distance over rough country would ever reach them.

There is also prevalent the idea that loneliness and isolation must mean unhappiness, which I do not think is at all true. I cannot remember ever meeting any man who lived such a life and who complained of it, or seemed at all unhappy. Indeed, shepherds and others I have known who lived a lonely life have all impressed me with their obvious contentment ; and the memory of four years in Western Canada, during which I was often alone for a week or more without even seeing a fellow human being, is a distinctly happy one.

Sometimes I think that if it were possible for country folk to obtain a living and at the same time to be left undisturbed by outside influences how blissful life in our countryside would be. Science and invention have given mankind great boons, no doubt, but they have largely taken from him that precious thing, privacy ; and before long he will realize his loss and demand that something be done about it. But what can be done ? To be let alone— it does not seem much to ask, but in these days it seems impossible to obtain.

That last rather disgruntled note is, I think, the direct result of three days in London. Three days of an endless succession of people's faces and hurrying feet on all sides, to the continuous accompaniment of mechanical noise. It was with a thankful heart that I woke up in rural Wilts the following morning.

And then, at ten a.m. a London friend rang me up. You see, one cannot be let alone for long. Business finished, he asked how the countryside was looking. Before replying I glanced out of the window of my study, and then said, " It's green with a background of clean sweet mist. Within twenty yards of this telephone there's a cow and calf in the farm yard, the wise head of my old hunter poking out over the half door of his box, and a starling chuckling on the stable roof. You can keep your old London, and welcome." And then he called me a lucky devil, and rang off. We country folk should be ever grateful for our privileges.

*   *   *   *   *   *

What a wet world just now! Rivers higher than they have been for two years, and water everywhere. Old Dame Nature is averaging up our rainfall with a vengeance. And who should grumble? Certainly neither farmers nor countryfolk generally; although most of them have been saying awful things about the weather during the past fortnight or so. Which is perhaps understandable and very human, but also very unfair. The only way for any farmer to judge fairly whether our climate has been his friend or his enemy is to do so over a period of ten years; when he will be bound to admit that the weather has done him more good and less harm than has mankind or his own foolishness.

However, the almost continuous wet weather during the past fortnight has almost been partly responsible for one of my young men giving me a week's notice. He is just eighteen, and was second man in an outdoor dairy of seventy cows. Morning after morning during the early milking it has pelted with rain, and finally, I imagine, fell the last drop which broke the back of his resolve to become a head dairy-man. At least, this was the reason he gave me, but the real one was, I think, that he had attained that restless age when a young man wants to broaden his outlook. He has joined the army and I gave him a most excellent reference with sincerity and pleasure. But, such is the pull of England's countryside, that I will bet money, if we are both spared for ten years, that I shall see him back on the land once more. My present head dairyman is an ex-seventh Dragoons guardsman, so perhaps his tales of soldiering have resulted in him losing a good mate, me losing a good employee, and the army gaining a smart young man with some jump in him.

*   *   *   *   *   *

Work and weather and the fact that my riding companion is at school for five days a week have combined to make me miss my occasional day's hunting for some time, but the other day I heard a hunting tale, which, I think, will bear repetition. Most stories of this character tell of the discomfiture of the non-hunting man or woman, but this anecdote is definitely one up to the critics of hunting.

A rather precious young man from Chelsea went to stay with some friends in the country, and one night went out with them to dine at a neighbour's house. There the company were all hunting folk, and the poor lad found himself between two very hard-bitten middle-aged Dianas. During the meal one of these suddenly asked him very fiercely, " Do you hunt ?" Whereupon he stuttered, and said nervously, " Ye-e-s. But only when I've lost something !" The more I think of this, the more I chuckle at the aptness of his answer.

*   *   *   *   *   *

Most of the leaves have disappeared, and the countryside is a wet bare world just now, but here and there one sees a touch of colour in the woods. Possibly the birches have always shown such brilliance in the Autumn, but I cannot remember such a bright orange tint before. In sun or mist the birches are flaming in our southern woodlands, and the other night their gaudiness showed finely in the headlights of my car as I was driving home through a large wood. Indeed, so bright was their colour that occasionally it seemed as though Chinese lanterns had been hung in the brushwood.

Many of the arable fields are showing the pale almond green sheen of next year's wheat crop, and everywhere rooks and starlings are high busy. I like to watch the former when they are returning home to roost about four-thirty. Starlings fly in a mass like a black cloud, which swishes overhead so quickly. But rooks are individuals. Each one has his or her own particular ideas as to the best way of conquering a head wind or using a tail wind. Against a gale some fly close to the ground, while others tack like a sailing ship. When a bird has lost a wing or tail feathers he sometimes performs very curious antics. I can remember getting quite pally with one rook some years ago, who was minus most of his tail and several feathers from one wing. Usually he flew low and followed the contour of the land, taking advantage of every bit of shelter from the wind. Then, when he was forced to rise at a hedge or row of trees the gale would sometimes lift him like a kite. Then he would be blown backwards like a leaf for maybe a hundred yards. But invariably he recovered his balance, and came tacking and side-slipping towards home.

Rain is all very well, and I prefer to have too much rather than too little, but just at the moment I am more than ready to shout with those who say, " Too much is enough." Really, all that has been done on most farms. for the past fortnight has been for men to come in out of the wet. I am beginning to agree with the townsman who said that in a well-ordered world rain would fall only at night.

*   *   *   *   *   *

The other day I witnessed a film of the activities of the Fairbridge Farm School. In many ways this method seems to be the best way of handling migration from too thickly-populated old countries to too thinly-populated new ones. For this reason—the emigrants leave their native land at about ten years old or even younger.

The result of this is that almost invariably they are successes, and become good citizens of their new country. I do not suggest for one moment that this is because the Fairbridge authorities " get them young and treat them rough," although such handling has much to be said for it. The reason, I think, lies in the first part of the quotation— they get them young.

Life in a new country overseas can never be all beer and skittles, and is bound to have its periods of depression, hardship, and disappointment. These young settlers know of no other life, and so they battle through. The adult who emigrates suffers too often from home-sickness, and instead of gritting his teeth to overcome his new troubles, mourns and yearns for his old home. Which, while it may be very natural, cannot help him in his new life.

Sometimes, I think, when this question of emigration is considered, that people are too apt to forget the real reason why men and women left this country years ago and founded overseas Dominions. It was, I am convinced, because they were devilish uncomfortable here—so uncomfortable that they thought any change must be for the better.

To-day this is the most comfortable country in the world for all classes of society, and so, instead of our young men emigrating, many of those who have emigrated are returning home.

*   *   *   *   *   *

Dipping into an old favourite last week, " Wild Life in a Southern County," by Richard Jefferies, I came across the following :—

The joy in life of these animals—indeed, of almost all animals and birds in freedom—is very great. You may see it in every motion—in the lissom bound of the hare, the playful leap of the rabbit, the song that the lark and finch *must* sing ; the soft loving coo of the dove in the hawthorn ; the blackbird ruffling out his feathers on a rail. The sense of living—the consciousness of seeing and feeling—is manifestly intense in them all, and is in itself an exquisite pleasure. Their appetites seem ever fresh : they rush to the banquet spread by Mother Earth with a gusto that Lucullus never knew in the midst of his artistic gluttony———.

Not for one moment do I suggest that this is not true of animals and birds in freedom, but the behaviour the other day of my daughter's pony and my ancient hunter told me that it can be true of animals in captivity. Owing to rain they had not been out for a good gallop for three days, and they just revelled in the chance. Not from vice nor from naughtiness did they misbehave, but from sheer joy of living. I must confess that I was nearly caught out. Thinking that my old horse was past such childish practices I was enjoying the sight of my daughter's pony putting his head down and bucking for pure pleasure, when all of a sudden I discovered that I also was seated on a jumping cracker. However, I just managed to stay there, and soon afterwards we had them going in fine style. I am always sorry for the horse which has to pull heavy loads at a slow speed—it seems to be such a monotonous toil—but I refuse to believe that the saddle horse and the fast trapper do not

enjoy their work at least as often as most human beings enjoy theirs.

    *   *   *   *   *   *

Looking at a map of this island which showed the political character of different districts as evinced by the recent election I could not help but notice that the Socialist element is strongest in our large cities and more thickly-populated areas.

Is this because modern civilization has almost completely divorced so many of these people from natural things ? Somehow I think this condition has much to do with mankind's political beliefs. Townsfolk generally live a life in which everything is ordered by man, and in which nothing just happens in God's good time. In consequence they are more ready to think everything can be put right by man's handiwork—if you like, they have complete faith in logic.

But life isn't logical, and no one realizes this essential truth more than the countryman. In his daily life there are so many things which cannot be ordered by man, things which just happen in spite of him, and in consequence he believes in magic and uses logic as a tool. His political attitude therefore is that legislation should confirm public opinion rather than lead it, while his town cousin is rather apt to think in exactly opposite fashion. In other words life is far more like poker than chess, and to live it successfully necessitates a natural flair, which only a natural life can give.

So, in spite of our large towns and our modern industrialism, the city socialism of to-day only becomes law when the countryside confirms it to-morrow, or rather some twenty years afterwards. Still, we must have reformers to bring these new ideas forward, and there is no doubt in my opinion that the recent increase of Socialist M.P.'s in in our Parliament will be all to the good for both town and country.

*   *   *   *   *   *

For some time now I have been convinced that for a hybrid being such as I, half-farmer and half-writer, the Winter is the best season for the latter activity. In the Summer there is so much to do and to enjoy out of doors that writing is often a penance, sometimes like a schoolboy's imposition and always like his prep. But now, when the days are short, when the wind and rain sweep round the house, the cosiness of my study after supper seems to make writing less of a task and more of a pleasure. The curtains are drawn, the house is quiet, and a log fire is such a helpful companion. In such a setting how much easier is it to shake out the wings of thought and let one's mind travel wide and far !

But always I am conscious that I have a farm, and that its Wiltshire acres should be credited with most of the output of my typewriter. And should I sometimes forget this, the farm has a clever habit of reminding me.

The other night at 11.30 p.m. a tap came at my window I drew the curtain and looked out to see a very good neighbour, who lives almost next door. One of my cows had got out, he told me, and so together we drove her into the farmyard, and shut the gates. Then, after thanking him and wishing him good-night, I returned indoors and worked until nearly 2 a.m.

*   *   *   *   *   *

In Winter, when the fields are white,
I sing this song for your delight

The High Road and the Low

For one whole week I have seen neither my farm nor my typewriter, having been away doing two jobs of work in Bonnie Scotland. True, the work was accomplished in one half day—twenty minutes in Broadcasting House, Edinburgh, during the afternoon, and a delightful and instructive two hours with that city's University's Agricultural Society the same evening—so, had I travelled by train, I could have managed the whole business in three days quite easily. Also, as every member of my family was at pains to point out very clearly, the train would have been safer and cheaper than a car. Their consideration for my person and pocket was most touching ; but, in spite of it or perhaps because of it, I drove up to Edinburgh by car, the reason being that I wanted to see the country. What farmer does not enjoy doing that ?

One learns all sorts of things from a long lonely journey of this kind. For instance, long before I reached Scotland I had decided that although this island looks quite small on a map of the world it is quite a chunk of land to drive over. My speedometer made it four hundred and fifty odd miles from Wiltshire to Edinburgh, and by the time the last mile was ticked off I had had enough and to spare of motoring for a while. Someday I intend to do that drive during summertime, and so be able to see and to admire the countryside when it is garbed in its heaviest clothing. But I'm not so sure that a farmer cannot see more of the real country at this time of the year. Its winter nakedness exposes its faults unmercifully.

One obtains curious impressions as one passes swiftly through strange country. Natives and lovers of the Shires will cry " Shame " on me, doubtless, but somehow I felt that all was far from well with this part of England from a farming point of view. It is, of course, unfair to pass judgment from such a cursory glance, but that is the impression which Leicestershire left upon me. I hope that I'm hopelessly wrong, for the land is good, gutty stuff ; which must mean, if I'm right, that mankind is hopelessly at fault. I was talking of this to a friend yesterday, and he asked me if I had ever noticed that where Nonconformity was strong the farming was always well done, and that where the Church of England flourished the reverse was the case. I am not qualified to give an opinion either way, but I shall make it my business to consider this argument wherever I travel in future. Memories of Cornish agriculture cause me furiously to wonder whether my friend may not be correct.

In contrast with the hunting Shires, Yorkshire showed me that it was farmed well. In fact, as one gets further north it becomes increasingly difficult to pick holes in the farming. Also in Yorkshire I saw something which made me think that we in the south of England are more slothful than our farming friends in that county. For at four o'clock, when it was so dark that one could not see from one end of the field to the other, I saw teams of horses plodding patiently along in front of the plough with an equally patient man or lad plodding steadfastly behind them. At such a time nearly every farm horse in Wiltshire would have been back in stable for at least an hour.

But possibly some of my criticisms of the Shires and my corresponding admiration for Yorkshire farming is because I found the landscape more attractive in that county. To me, a downsman, the Shires are too flat, too stolid, and too lacking in background. In them one cannot lift one's heart to the everlasting hills; because there ain't any hills. Farther north, even where the hills are missing, there is a fine roll to the countryside, which I found most attractive and I was sorry when night hid it from my sight.

The word " stolid " in the previous paragraph seems to be the best adjective for the Shires. In good times for beef production I can imagine no pleasanter place to farm, and I have a notion that the Shire farmers did pretty well without overworking themselves very much during the first twenty years of the twentieth century. The sun shone the rain came down, the grass grew, their beasts got fat, and the price of beef brought enough to pay all expenses and leave a bit over for hunting. But such placidity over a generation does not tend to equip farmers to face bad times and changing methods. Professor Stapledon mourns that war-time exigencies did not enable the plough to bite into the permanent pasture of the shires ; but, although I admit the force of his argument that such a happening would have helped that district's farming to face the recent depression, I cannot say that I should like to see that lovely grassland turned into arable.

Just after lighting-up time, the rain came down to interrupt my musings—not just a shower but a downpour. I thought of the Yorkshire ploughmen whom I had just passed, and gave thanks to the inventors of saloon bodies for cars. Still the rain belted down, so I gave up hope of reaching Newcastle, and hunted and found most admirable shelter for man and car at Boroughbridge. And did I sleep well ? Anyone who has driven over 250 miles in a day knows the answer.

* * * * * *

God made the county of Durham, and since then man has done his best to spoil it. At least, that was my impression as I drove through it next morning. That there is beautiful countryside to be found in Durham I have no doubt, for since my return one Durham farmer has written me to that effect, and very kindly invited me to call some day to have a look at it. Next time I make this journey I shall take him at his word.

But up to date I have seen hardly any countryside in this county worth looking at. Coal and iron we must have I know, and in the past their getting has been profitable to both getters and users ; but what a mess their getting means ! Mr. J. B. Priestly points this out admirably in his book, " English Journey ". Much money has been taken from this district, he says, and spent elsewhere in all sorts of ways ; but the mess caused in its taking has been left behind. That this is a crime which man's civilization has committed against the people and the countryside of Durham admits of no denial ; and as yet the criminal has made no adequate atonement.

Recently, industry has been and still is moving south, but every southerner should make a trip through some of our northern black country. What the eye does not see the heart does not grieve over, and no newspaper report can bring the tragedy of our northern industrial districts home to those of us who live and work in the sunny south. By comparison we know nothing of bad times or of unemployment, and a sight of it at first hand shakes one's equanimity. At least it has shaken mine, but like most folk I hurried away from such unpleasant thoughts and scenes as quickly as possible. I am no speed merchant, but I will confess that I was coward enough to put my foot hard down at every possible opportunity during my journey through Durham.

But once Newcastle with its traffic was left behind, and the bonnet of my car was headed for Otterburn, I felt better. Northumberland is, I think, one of the most beautiful and one of the greatest farming counties in England. To any of my Wiltshire farming friends I would say this, " If you want to see how pastures should be grown and handled, take a trip to Northumberland." And here I must apologize to one farmer in that county for trespassing upon his domain. But I just couldn't help it. No farmer so far north had any right to have such a green pasture in December. So I pulled up, and trespassed for a quarter of an hour, " for to see and to admire." Perhaps here it would be only fitting to give honour where honour is due, and to say that the beneficial effect of the education and research of Armstrong College is printed plain on Northumberland's fair countryside for he who trespasses as I did to read.

Hitherto I had been travelling through a green and brown England, and thinking that the tales of the rigour of the northern climate were but fiction ; but, as soon as Otterburn was passed, I struck Winter in his mantle of snow. Soon the road was merely two black streaks in a white world. A wise man would have turned back while there was yet time, but a fool such as I, having decided to enter Scotland by way of Carter Bar, continued northwards. Soon, on the last petrol pump in England, I passed a most sinister notice, which warned me that the first petrol pump in Scotland was 21 miles ahead. This did not look as though those miles would be very thickly inhabited, but as my tank contained ample for the car to cover them, I drove steadily onwards.

Soon I was forced to realize three uncomfortable things—firstly, that the only way to avoid being ditched was to go very slowly ; secondly, that to turn back was impossible ; and thirdly, that if I once stopped I should very likely be unable to get going again. But it is wonderful what the modern car can tackle, and slowly did it that day. One car crawling up a narrow track between two white-sheeted hills. Away to the left I could see occasional farmhouses and steadings, and the blue curl of smoke coming from the chimneys. What a lonely life their occupants must live, I thought, and yet, in spite of the wild and deserted nature of the country I felt that I should not mind living in such a setting.

Two or three years ago I was privileged to visit a farmer in this county during December, and I was struck, not only with the isolation of his home, but also with the completeness of his life. His farm seemed to provide him with every possible need—meat, eggs, milk, fuel, sport, bread, and even blankets made from the wool of his own sheep. What more can man desire ? Think how snug one would sleep between blankets from one's own flock !

But, of course, food and clothing and sport are not everything—a man must drink. Well, very certainly his farm provided a copious supply of sparkling water ; and surely a little drop of something stronger could be brewed or distilled as occasion required ? But to do either is perhaps illegal. Well, what of it ? I should doubt very much that man's town law runs in lovely wild Northumberland during wintertime. And when I recall the merry red face and twinkling eyes of that particular farmer, I feel sure that in the matter of drinking he obeys no law save his own.

Slowly but not exactly surely I crept upwards to Carter Bar. The highest chalk hill in England is Inkpen Beacon in Hampshire, 1,011 feet, and I had reckoned that Carter Fell, 2,020 feet, would provide a contrast. And it did !

I felt very small as I neared the Bar, and was very glad to see a man clearing a drift of snow on the crest of the hill. Thanks to his work that morning I was able triumphantly to put uphill behind me and to slide very very slowly indeed downhill into Scotland, and to stop for a much-needed late lunch at Jedburgh.

*   *   *   *   *   *

Having conquered Carter Bar in snow, and with a good lunch under my belt, I set out from Jedburgh, thinking that the remainder of my journey to Edinburgh would be easy. The snow soon disappeared, and I was able to slip along in great style. Edinburgh by four o'clock, said I to myself, said I.

And then somewhere about half-way between Jedburgh and Edinburgh, I struck mountains and snow once more. But still there seemed to be nothing to worry about. This road was used, and I was continually meeting cars. Evidently such winter conditions were child's play to these hardy Scots. Ah well, here a southerner would show them that he also could face their snow-covered roads.

Alas ! A hundred yards ahead of me on an ice-covered slope was a lorry, travelling towards Edinburgh. Suddenly at a bend, I saw it falter, stop, and slip sideways and backwards in drunken fashion. Needless to say I stopped. My invasion of Scotland was a friendly one, and I had no desire either to kill or be killed. But for a moment I feared for that lorry driver and for myself, and I was glad when his lorry came to rest diagonally across the road.

In ten minutes time there was a line of halted cars behind me, and their drivers and I walked, or rather skated up the hill to help. A roadman threw down some grit with a shovel, and we all shoved. After about half an hour of this we managed to get the lorry moving, and soon that hillside was bare of cars once more. An hour later I was recounting my adventures to my host and hostess, and listening to their plans for my three day visit.

*   *   *   *   *   *

I can remember a town friend asking me why it was that the countryman would rarely give a decided opinion about anything. I replied that it was because in his daily life there were so few things which were entirely under man's power to control—the weather, for instance. When asked about the probabilities of to-morrow's weather the Wiltshire peasant says, " I 'low 'twill rain." Or " Gwaine to be fine termorrer, 'twillably." That last word is either a contraction of " most probably " or of " I believe," and everyday some of my men use it in conversation with me. They say that something willably, doably, or shallably, but never, never, never will they commit themselves by saying that anything will or shall or does. Why ? Just because they know better than to prophesy what Nature will or will not do ; a characteristic, which, while it may be sound, can be and often is very annoying.

It was a remark of the stranded lorry driver which reminded me of this conversation. While we were fussing with his lorry, someone asked him what load he had aboard, and he answered ," Och ! Jist a wheen pigs fra marrrket." At least, that was what it sounded like to my unaccustomed ears, but even so, it did prove to me once again that one of

The High Road and the Low

the values of dialect speech is that it enables the listener to place the speaker. In addition, of course, all dialects have a rare descriptive quality, and are efficient methods of getting one's meaning across with the minimum of effort.

I said this one day to a friend who was and is a bit of a purist in speech, and he replied that dialect was plain proof of laziness on the part of its users. " They don't sound their aitches," he said. " They clip the ends of their words, they run two words together in most horrible fashion, and they use Z for S merely because it requires less effort to enunciate. Just laziness, pure and simple."

As I say, he was a purist ; so I told him the tale of how one purist met his death. It is a sad story, and should serve as a warning to any budding purists. He was in a nursing home recovering from an operation on his eyes, and his nurse, had to read to him. He chose a very highbrow book, which the poor girl found very dull. After reading for some time she asked the patient, " Whatever did you choose a book like that to be read to out of for ?" Four prepositions at the end of a sentence was too much for him, so he turned his face to the wall and died. Why, I don't know, for surely his nurse's meaning was plain, and surely to convey one's meaning is the main object of speech ?

It was a conversation with Grey Owl, which reminded me of this tale. I was privileged to meet him the other day at the Sunday Times Book Exhibition, where, incidentally, he stood out amongst the company as the most dignified looking person present. When I told him that I had spent four years in a shanty in N.W. Manitoba he thawed rapidly, and told me tales of his life and of his writings. One of his remarks sticks in my mind.

" They tell me that I split my infinitives," he said.

" Goldarn it ! I don't know what an infinitive is."

But this lack does not prevent him from being able to write interesting books, a fact which should give the purists something to think about. Too often the purist, while he may write good English, has nothing interesting to write about ; the reason being, I suppose, that he has spent all his life in keeping pure—always a dull business.

*   *   *   *   *   *

Just one more note about dialect. The use of the wrong word has always been recognized in this country as funny, and the other day I came across a new instance of this. I asked a rural builder just why he had purchased some derelict cottages which had been condemned as unfit for human habitation.

" I got a notion to turn 'em into garridges," he said. " Ye see, you kin do wot you likes wi' they dialect 'ouses."

Whether he can or not remains to be seen, but I'm not so sure that "dialect" was not quite as suitable an adjective as " derelict " to describe those cottages.

*   *   *   *   *   *

This particular trip to Scotland was not so " farmery " as last year's although it enabled me to meet many more Scottish farmers and budding farmers. But instead of meeting them one by one on their farms, I met them in the mass, first while lecturing at Edinburgh University and later the same evening at the Scottish Factors' Annual Dinner, two functions which I thoroughly enjoyed. I hope that I did nothing at either to lessen the enjoyment of others. Never have I lectured to an audience which was so alive, so keen, and so good tempered withal ; and never have I sat at dinner with more generous hosts or more entertaining companions.

For the remainder of my stay I played indifferent but very pleasant golf and bridge ; but on the one full day's golf—all I could manage—I nearly disgraced myself. My host was under contract to listen to an address on the I.L.O. immediately after tea that day, and when I confessed that I did not know what the I.L.O. was he hurried me through our afternoon round so that my education should be improved. Incidentally, I don't think he was quite sure what those three mystic letters stood for.

Two rounds at Muirfield in a December wind, while they are very conducive to sleep, are hardly the best preparation for listening to lectures, interesting as this one was. I had a dickens of a job to keep awake, and it was only when I noticed my host in similiar case on the platform, that I forgave him for placing me in the front row of the audience. However, as a result, both he and I know a lot more about the work of the International Labour Office than we did before.

What can one say of such a short time in Scotland ? Oh, any amount ! Of the people, to give the lie to two popular expressions, by stating that Scottish folk are the reverse of mean, and that they have a keener appreciation of humour than the average Englishman of my acquaintance. The popular thing is, of course, to remark that they are better educated. That is as it may be, but one result of their education is that they are less hide-bound than my own countrymen, especially in their attitude to political questions and farming problems. Should any of them read the following sentence how they will chuckle in amazement! But honesty insists that it must be written—open confession being good for even a southerner's soul.

In Scotland it is possible to be an avowed supporter

of any particular political faith without one's neighbours of a different faith looking upon you as a lost soul. In Scotland anyone, even a farmer, can be an avowed Socialist without being looked upon as a danger to the community and being treated as a pariah. Although, as yet, I am not a Socialist, I cannot help writing, "England's rural districts, please copy." Such a sane and broadminded social and political atmosphere amply compensates for any climatic disadvantages from which Scotland may suffer by comparison with the sunny south of England.

Of the farming one can only write in praise and admiration. Granted the Lothian farmers have marvellous land, and most of the Border sheep men are large capitalists; but, by comparison with either, I must confess that we southerners are slovens. Of course, every district discovers the type of farming best suited to its natural characteristics, and doubtless our southern slovenly methods are the most economic for this part of England, but once again I take my hat off to the Scots.

But enough of this humility! It is high time a southerner kept his end up. In gaol or in London the correct thing to say, of course, is " I think your policemen just wonderful." In Scotland surely one should say the same about the golf courses? Which I can say with truth, but here is the joke against the Scots. Twice have I visited Scotland, and six or seven rounds of golf have I played there. By the mercy of Providence, a power which justly rewarded my humble bearing in that stern and wild country, I have yet to be beaten at golf on Scottish soil.

But what a fall awaits me when next I journey north! Who cares? Sufficient for this trip was the triumph thereof!

I did not attempt to tackle Carter Bar on my journey home as there was still far too much snow in South Scotland to make motoring a pleasure. Instead, I took the coast road, and travelled without incident into England. But at Morpeth disaster almost overtook me, and to add to my shame, in a built-up area. Since leaving Berwick-on-Tweed I had been travelling well on a good road, from which the sun had melted the previous night's flit of snow ; and somehow or other I did not notice that the entrance to Morpeth from the north was in the shade. As I did no one any harm, and there were no witnesses of my escapade, if is safe to relate what happened. I, or rather my car, slid sideways into Morpeth, and came to rest with a bump against the near curb. Thereafter I drove very carefully on a snow-covered road all the way, and managed to reach Nottingham and bed without further incident.

Next morning I found more snow south of Nottingham, and it was not until I reached Oxfordshire that I saw the green and brown of farming once more. From that moment I was in familiar country, and very soon home to find Wiltshire looking much the same as when I had left it five days before. Land, thank God, stays put.

*   *   *   ·   *   *   *

Of all the many extraordinary things which have come my way since I stumbled into this writing game, the membership of a certain London Club is one of which I value the most. The kindly welcome which its habituées extended to a nervous farmer is something which I shall never forget and for which I shall be for ever grateful. Soon after I joined I wandered into the bridge room one afternoon, and sat watching a rubber. When it came to an end I was invited to cut in. At that date my knowledge of contract was of the slightest, so I confessed it, and suggested that the original four had best carry on. Whereupon one fierce but kindly individual said, " I have seen b———s like you before. You will play."

I have set that down in order to show the friendly welcome which I received, but what follows goes to show that the discipline of a club is a very valuable thing for the average man. For three years I never fell foul of it, being careful to realize that I was a very new boy in a very clever school ; but soon after my return from Scotland I was caught tripping.

I had spent the afternoon and evening in lecturing and debating farming policy with a gathering of farmers. I must confess that I was a trifle disappointed at the attitude of my audience. When one has spent considerable time in preparing a paper, one does not mind criticism or flat disagreement, but it does nark one to have the result of one's labours carefully talked out rather than discussed. Possibly the contrast between the attitudes of an English and Scottish audience had something to do with this. The latter wanted to discuss everything ; the former had made up their minds that everything was wrong, and that it would be dangerous to discuss the possibilities of any point being right.

Anyway, I was not in the best of humours when I left, and at ten-thirty that evening I turned into the bridge room of my club, where, I felt sure, the difference in the general atmosphere, would bring comfort. Immediately I was greeted with ribald queries as to where I had spent the evening, together with bawdy suggestions that the simple countryman had been ensnared by London's vice.

" Cheaper to lose money to us, farmer," was the general conclusion. Whereupon, without thinking, I said, " Well, if you must know what I've been at, I've been wrangling politics all the evening with a lot of farmers."

And then one of my friends, God bless him, cocked his eye at the company and said, "H'm ! Mark the class consciousness. Two years ago he wouldn't have put it like that."

How delicious ! How salutary ! And how very true ! Open confession is good for the soul. This new life of mine is making me forget that primarily I am a farmer. Two years ago I should not have put it like that. And I'll take damn good care that it will be more than another two years before my club friends see fit to reprove me so justly for that sort of thing again.

*   *   *   *   *   *

Rightly or wrongly I have always considered myself to be fairly progressive in my farming, but a visit to a friend's farm this afternoon has caused me furiously to think.

New and up-to-date implements were conspicuous by their absence. There was, it is true, a tractor, but I knew that this had been purchased only some six months before, and that it was the first implement of this type which my friend had ever owned or used. But, as we walked round his farm together, I was filled with admiration for the enormous imdrovement which he had effected in three or four years.

The fences were all good ; the fields were tidy ; even the fences round the hayricks were proof against any stock ; the whole place looked as though it was combed and brushed every day ; and, greatest improvement of all, there was not one rabbit on some seven hundred acres of rabbity country.

But from what I could hear or see there had been no modern method of rabbit extermination used. The farmer had walked round some two miles of rabbit wire on his boundary at least once daily, in order to stop even the beginnings of a breach in the ramparts ; the rabbits inside the boundary had been exterminated with pick and shovel by main strength ; and their burrows subsequently levelled and sown with grass seeds.

Tenacity of purpose was the chief weapon used against them ; and I gathered the impression that should one rash rabbit manage to invade the farm the combined forces of the whole staff would have been turned on him forthwith. Quite frankly, my friend can justly claim the title of " Rabbits' Enemy, Number One."

And that, I think, is the key to farming prosperity— tenacity of purpose. This quality is superior to any purchased implement. Of course, where one finds modern methods allied to it the result is all to the good ; but far too often the former seem to be used as a means whereby the farmer can spend more time away from his farm.

What I mean is this. A tractor is a good implement ; so is a milking machine ; artificial manures properly used are profitable ; and so are all the discoveries of science and invention ; but without the continued presence of the farmer on the farm their usefulness is divided by ten. With or without up-to-date methods the farmer who walks round his farm twice daily on his two flat feet will weather any depression better than the man who, no matter how modern his equipment, performs this important duty say only once

The master's foot is the best dung

a week. Even to-day the old proverb holds good—" The master's foot is the best dung."

My friend evidently agrees with this view, for, when I asked him if he saw much of a young couple who had recently taken the farm next to his, he looked across the valley towards their farmhouse and said, " No. Beats me what they want a house for.   They're never there."

The whole trend of these notes seems to be in direct opposition to the current notions concerning successful farming ; but I came away from my friend's farm feeling so humble and and so ashamed of myself that I have been carefully considering the problem from this angle. Every influence to-day seems to be urging the farmer to adopt new methods and to invest in new aids in his business. Be up-to-date or perish is the modern cry. But when I think of all the many farmers whom I have known more or less intimately, I am forced to admit that their success varies in direct relationship to the measure of their resistance to the forces which urge the immediate adoption of the latest scientific method or most recent invention.

Such a conclusion must be an incorrect one, I suppose ; but the devil of it is that the more I consider it the more correct it seems. Doubtless this confession will bring much scathing criticism upon my head ; but I would ask any critic to review the success or failure of his farming acquaintances carefully before he decides that I am talking utter nonsense.

In addition I hope that no one will think that I am against new methods or up-to-date implements. On the contrary, I am merely suggesting that their adoption or purchase on the part of the farmer should be considered as important a thing as marriage—that is to say, not to be taken in hand lightly or unadvisedly. In other words, in this connection very often fools rush in where angels fear to tread. And incidentally I have a notion that it is a rare occurrence for anyone to refer to farmers as angels.

*   *   *   *   *   *

After many heartsearchings and—neither of us being ashamed to admit it—some tears, Pam and I have said good-bye to Toby. A lady friend has offered to lend Pam a cob of 14.2 for a year, and it seemed too good an offer to refuse. So one day last week he arrived by train, and was met at the station by the whole establishment. His name is Tommy, but we have christened him Tom Webster, for his face and expression are exactly like those of the horses in the *Daily Mail* Cartoons which bear the same signature. The morning after his arrival we clipped him, and tried him out. He proved eminently satisfactory in every way, so a home had to be found for Toby.

This was a difficult business. Firstly, Toby had to be sold to a good home ; secondly, to a home near by, where he could be visited by his former mistress ; and thirdly, to a buyer who would promise not to resell him for at least a year. To Pam's great joy one of my near neighbours bought Toby as a first pony for his little girl, one of Pam's school friends, so everybody is happy, save Pam's mother. The trouble is that Pam has already discovered that Master Thomas Webster likes jumping, and in consequence her mother fears the worst. And incidentally so does her father. He could follow Toby anywhere without much difficulty, but this cob's performances are causing him considerable concern.

*   *   *   *   *   *

At the moment my telephone is half out of order. Although other folk can ring me up, I cannot ring up anyone. Here let me hasten to say that this is not because I have not paid my account, but because the flood water down the road has managed to effect this one way traffic of speech.

The result is damnable. Anyone and everyone can and do ring me up, and I am unable to retaliate in kind. Was ever a man so harassed by modern invention ?

So the other night in a fit of childish bad-temper I went to bed early, and swore that if anyone rang up they jolly well could. I had the beginnings of a cold, a fit of the blues, writing had gone badly and farming worse all day, and it was still raining.

At ten o'clock, just as I was in my first sleep, the telephone rang. I let it ring. It rang again at 10.30, at 11.0, and at 11.30 ; and each time I let it ring and snuggled a trifle more deeply beneath the bed clothes. Obviously it was an important call—somebody dead, somebody dying, or someone with some urgent business. But that was three nights ago and as yet I have not found out who it was or what it was. Which just shows you how wise I was to lie snug that night.

Honours between myself and the telephone are now easy, I consider ; but how I wish it would stop raining !

*   *   *   *   *   *

Christmas and the New Year

During my lifetime I have spent the evening of Christmas Eve in all sorts of places—alone in a shanty in North-West Manitoba ; drinking far too much alcohol in a hotel in Shoal Lake, a little wet town (by wet I mean that it had a licence) in the same province ; sitting up in a draughty Wiltshire stable with a sick horse ; and once, when Christmas Eve fell on a Saturday, in wrestling with the weekly dairy books of my retail milk rounds until one o'clock on Christmas morning. But this year I spent Christmas Eve around midnight in the most curious place imaginable.

Somewhere in the bowels of the earth underneath Broadcasting House I helped a gathering of most cheery folk to wish the listeners in the British Empire a Merry Christmas. Apparently the idea was to give them a taste of as many Old Country Christmas flavours as possible. There was a piper in kilts to tell them that Scotland still stood where it did ; a Chelsea pensioner to assure them that honoured old age was not forgotten at Christmastide ; a sailor to give greetings to those afloat ; singers, musicians, and speakers of every type imaginable ; and a jazz band to garnish the whole dish.

In the midst of this galaxy of talent Mr. Howard Marshall and myself were down to do our little bit. For some seven or eight minutes we were to discuss the relative advantages of town and country as a setting for the Christmas holiday, Mr. Marshall to boost the town and I to stick up for the country. He and I had a confab in the ante-room a few minutes before entering the studio, and doped out the argument. It struck me as rather curious that the champion of the town should confess to having a car outside in Langham Place, and to the intention of streaking out into the country for Christmas as soon as our show was over ; the more especially as I, the supporter of the country, was unable to get home until next morning.

When we had agreed the line of our argument we entered the studio, and I must confess that I nearly laughed aloud at what I saw and heard there. A young lady in a business-like soprano was informing the Empire that it was her lucky star, and that she loved it from afar. Accompanying her was the jazz orchestra, its powers muted to a discreet pum-pum in time with the tune. But in the last chorus both the singer and the members of the band woke to life. The singer swept into that chorus on the flood-tide of a full orchestra. She insisted that the Empire was her lucky star, and right nobly did the musicians agree with her. In shirt sleeves—it was hot down there in that studio—the conductor urged them to still greater frenzy. The saxophones wailed like lost souls ; the drummer hit all sorts of things at one and the same time ; like automatons the wielders of the banjos thrummed out the beat ; and through all this cacophony the singer loved the Empire from afar with almost unmaidenly fervour—much too heady stuff for such young and immature nations.

Then, at a signal from the conductor, the clamour ceased, as suddenly as though its cords, or rather chords, had been severed by a sharp knife ; and a silence ensued which could almost be felt. In the midst of it all the musicians looked around in that self-satisfied fashion which is the habit of this particular species of human beings when any number of them manage, by luck or judgment, to bring their musical hubbub to a neat and crisp ending.

Now that particular type of finish to a piece of music, of which modern bands are so inordinately proud, has been the fashion in rural circles since time out of mind, at pig club dinners, harvest suppers, and even in " Terrier " regimental messes. Down in Wilts, whenever we sing " The vly be on the turmut," usually without a conductor, we always finish in similar style ; the second syallable of the final " turmut " being signalled by the simultaneous crash of numerous tankards and glasses upon the table. And woe betide the man who is late. Such a *faux pas* costs him a round of drinks, for the countryside still educates its children by an enforced appreciation of cause and effect. I am glad to think that the modern town dance band has attained almost to the precision of the countryside in musical matters.

However, it ill becomes me to criticize those musicians in that studio. Having finished their devotions for the moment, they now sat up to listen to Mr. Marshall and myself. Nonchalantly we two experienced broadcasters advanced to the microphone. A seven minute debate was child's play to us. Alas for our nonchalance. In a few seconds we had forgotten the meaning of the word. We expected to be announced in suitably dignified fashion, and then to speak our little piece. But we had forgotten the Christmas spirit. This had so overcome our announcer friend, also in shirt sleeves, that he gaily announced us to the mighty British Empire on which the sun never sets as a couple of cross talk comedians ! ! !

Having done his worst he backed away from the microphone, and waved us to carry on. For one split second we gaped at each other, and then, forgetting our carefully-prepared notes, we ragged each other unmercifully. What we said I cannot now remember, but everyone present seemed to be highly amused, and it is to be hoped that the Empire followed suit. In fact, such is the conceit of human nature, that I have been fancying myself as a comedian ever since. In the hope that these lines may catch Mr. Marshall's eye I here suggest to him that we should abandon our former broadcasting roles, and take up this cross-talk comedy business ; for, of course, a stupendous fee per minute, as laughter pays better than either tears or common-sense in all walks of life.

But, of course, we shall not obtain permission. That is the worst of making a do of any particular line of the entertainment business — the powers that be make you stick to your last. Indeed, with regard to books, rumour hath it that the author of the Vicar of Wakefield experienced the same difficulty. He suggested to his publishers that he should follow it up with a thriller, whereupon they took him out to lunch and told him firmly that his next book must be entitled " The Curate of Stow on the Wold."

So, no doubt Mr. Marshall will continue to tell us just how well Harold Larwood is bowling, and I shall be asked to carry on with the dispensing of rural charm ; and both of us are and should be thankful that we have the opportunity so to do. But when I think of that rib-shattering cross-talk act which the world will never hear tears come to my eyes. Think how splendidly we could be billed—Oward and Harthur ! And when television arrives—but no ! Modesty forbids.

*   *   *   *   *   *

For the first time in my life I woke up in London on Christmas morning, and I did not get home until one o'clock in the afternoon ; and thereafter it rained and it rained and it rained. And now that Christmas has come and gone it is still raining, and the New Year weeps as though it could never be comforted. At the moment there is four feet of clear spring water in the cellar directly underneath the floor of my study, and I can hear its continuous gurglings as I write. There is also a good foot of water covering the road past the farmhouse for nearly two hundred yards ; sufficient water in the piggeries and stables to make it necessary to remove their inhabitants to drier quarters ; dire stories—I hope exaggerated somewhat —of the amount of water up the valley ; and a weeping sky overhead.

My particular trouble is that the rivers Wylye and Till join forces a mile or two above my farm ; that on its way to the sea at Christchurch every drop of their total output has to flow through my native town of Wilton ; and that a considerable portion of this must, perforce, flow through or rather over my farm. In effect this means that we have to deal with all the water which falls on the Wylye valley between Warminster and Wilton, plus a goodly share of that which falls on Salisbury Plain. For just now every " Winter Bourne " is living up to its name and the oh so dry ditch of summer is now a raging torrent.

When it gets really going either fire, flood or tempest makes man's efforts to stop it appear very feeble and inadequate. Indeed, I am convinced that to try to stop flood water is to accentuate the trouble in most instances. The water is up the valley, and it must come down its appointed pathway to the sea ; and in my experience

sooner is usually a lot better than later. In other words I
agree with my " drowner," who told me one day last week
that he was driven out of his beloved " medders " by the
water, and that " 'twerden no good to do nothin' else but
let it goo."

Adults may detest a flood, but how children enjoy it!
My small daughter has been compelled by an irate mother
to change her stockings at least four times daily, for no
Wellington boot is proof against her activities in the flood
outside the house. And all day long there is a crowd of
happy children on the raised pavement of planks, splashing
and making merry, and incidentally laying up a goodly
store of colds for the near future. There is also one other
inhabitant of the farm who is enjoying the present conditions. Somehow or other one lone duck escaped execution
at Christmas, and just now she is enjoying herself tremendously on the lake which represents the farmyard. It is her
first taste of natural conditions, and the edict has gone forth
that she is not to die until the floods have abated.

It is at times like this that I give especial thanks for
Open-Air Milking. Granted, this wet winter has been the
reverse of helpful for this method of dairying, but when I
think of the days when I had sixty cows to handle in flooded
buildings and yards I realize the advantages of my present
system. Also I know that the cattle are healthier on the
top of the downs—in spite of the mud even up there—than
they would be down in a flooded world, both indoors and
out. And here I must take off my hat to those stalwarts
who have worked the bail so manfully—and what is perhaps
even more important, so cheerfully — during the recent
continuous wet weather.

But enough of grousing about the weather. Every type

has its advantages as well as its disadvantages ; and from a farming point of view I prefer rain, flood even, to either frost or drought. It is possible to ride in the rain, and so for three reasons I took a day off yesterday, and went hunting. The first was because it was the last chance for my daughter this holiday ; the second because I wanted badly to get away from my desk for a whole day—that is the beauty of hunting, one gets right away for several hours ; and the third for health's sake, my increasing avoirdupois being an ever-present worry.

We had a really good day, and I bucketed my sixteen stone and far too evident tummy for a good twenty miles before it was over. Result—a feeling of well-being this morning, which, although I am a trifle stiff all over, is very welcome.

*   *   *   *   *   *

Just two fine days, which, much to every adult's relief, made the floods subside a trifle, and then snow, frost, and a biting north-east wind over the week end. Yesterday afternoon, Sunday, I drove with a neighbour some thirty miles in order to visit a dealer friend in North Wilts. For the first ten miles or so of the journey the roads themselves were clear of snow, although the countryside on either side was white with it ; but afterwards we came to snow-covered roads, and had to go cautiously.

There is no doubt that the northern half of Wilts always experiences a harder winter than does the south of the county, for I can remember that even in my boyhood Dauntsey's School and its surroundings were always much colder than the farmhouse at home. In case anyone should think I am suggesting that the school was not properly warmed in those far off days, let me hasten to say that I am referring solely to the difference in climatic conditions outdoors. It may be that the many improvements which have taken place at the school since my day have necessitated the removal of the hot pipes which ran along under the wall of the then dining hall. But I have vivid memories of sitting on them with my trousers tightly stretched over my hams, and of savouring that delicious moment just before the heat-engendered pain became too intense to be borne for another second.

School memories are rarely concerned with education, but usually with odd things like hot water pipes, incidents connected with games, or with the memory of one's half-starved condition from the first day of term until the last. Why is it that from thirteen to sixteen the male of human species is always hungry ? And what a just retribution overtakes most men in middle-age, when they are so fond of telling the present boys at their old school harrowing tales of the hardships which they suffered in connection with the school rations of years ago. After forty most of them are concerned with their waist-lines ; pay doctors good money to tell them what not to eat ; and are forced to do physical exercises in the bathroom before breakfast. To all three I plead guilty.

But at school I was always hungry, and on one never-to-be-forgotten occasion I fell foul of authority because of my gluttony. On two days a week, Tuesdays and Fridays I think, we were allowed to buy eggs, write our names on them, and leave them on a tray to be boiled for our teas. To me and many others this was a heaven-sent opportunity to satisfy our gnawing stomachs ; and when eggs were cheap — occasionally they were twenty-four a shilling — we took full advantage of it.

Alas ! The practice became too popular, and we overdid it until one day when the Head came in to the hall at tea-time, and said,

" A curious phenomenon has occurred. We have, the matron tells me, eighty-four egg cups. There are seventy boys sitting down to tea, and I see that there are dozens of eggs without a cup. Will all those boys who are so greedy that they have put in more than one egg come to see me in my study before prayers ! "

Needless to say I was amongst the culprits who visited his sanctum, but, thanks be, the good man never imagined any greater gluttony than two eggs per boy, and did not ask us to confess to actual numbers. For I and several others had from four to six each to our credit ! Such greed would have deserved expulsion in his eyes, I fear.

One other memory of school feeding comes to my mind. We groused, as boys have done and will continue to do all down the ages, about the school grub when we were home for the holidays ; only to be told, quite truthfully, by our parents that we looked extraordinarily well on it. Where-upon my brother explained the reason beautifully.

" You don't understand, Mother," he said. " At school we are taught the rationing of livestock, and all about albuminoids and carbohydrates. For illustration we are fed on scientific lines. We get just enough, but no more."

Which, undoubtedly, we did.

$$* \qquad * \qquad * \qquad * \qquad * \qquad *$$

For some time now I have become more and more convinced that owner-occupiers — provided they have adequate capital—can farm more profitably than tenant farmers. They can plan all their improvements with an eye to nothing save their own profit ; and, what is more important, effect these improvements immediately they become necessary. The same applies to any change in their methods of farming to suit any marked change in public taste or world conditions.

One owner-occupier has admitted this to me, and he went even further, saying that the thing for a farmer to buy was land which had no archaic encumbrances upon it. By archaic encumbrances he said that he did not mean tithe, but existing fences, wells, farmhouses, and buildings. "Such things cramp your style," he explained. "No matter how much you fight against it, you will find that you are suiting your modern farming to the old-fashioned and therefore inefficient equipment which you have bought with the land. What you want to do is to buy a farm of, say, five hundred acres, sell the house and buildings and a small paddock or two to a retired admiral, build a small modern house for yourself, and then equip the remaining land with what your farming needs, and nothing else."

I pass on this advice for two reasons. Firstly, because I have seen the speaker's balance sheet and it has made me green with envy ; and secondly, because I am convinced that in the remark which I have quoted is contained much of the art and mystery of successful farming in these difficult days.

I was talking in this strain to a town friend the other day, and he asked me whether I knew of any instances where a man had started in farming from small beginnings and achieved any appreciable financial success. Another farmer friend of mine was present, and we immediately grinned at each other, and proceeded to enumerate the men we knew who had performed this difficult feat. The two cases which staggered our town friend the most were those in which we vouched that the men who were now worth several thousand pounds apiece had been farm employees earning fourteen shillings a week only twenty years ago. We tried to explain that the recipe used in each case had been a suitable mixture of hard work, common sense, thrift, and tenacity of purpose. However, he doubted the efficacy of these qualifications to produce such a transformation in the financial standing of their possessors, and said,

" Of course, the recent policy will have helped them considerably."

" Not by a jugful," cut in my friend. " Those fellows knew better than to grow wheat. Instead they bought it. They've got on in spite of the policy. They fought for themselves. The Government help 'em ? I tell you no government could stop 'em."

*   *   *   *   *   *

Isn't it queer that the countryman who has succeeded by his allegiance to individualism and capacity to fight for himself almost invariably tries to get his offspring into a salaried job where such qualities must be " cribbed, cabined, and confined " by regimentation and government regulation ?

I met a farmer the other day who informed me with pride that his son was at a university and that if all went well he would become a school teacher. He said that at school the lad had shown a capacity to pass examinations, and that because of this, in spite of bad times, he had stinted himself in order that his son should be able to give this bent full play. I knew that this farmer had given up hunting, shooting, and every form of luxury and amusement for the past ten years, and, although I could well understand that he was happy and proud to have done this for his son, I was rather hurt at his attitude to his own calling. Both he and his son seemed so very convinced that to become a teacher was a great step upwards from farming.

Teaching and farming are great and very necessary professions, but I should question whether the former has any right to pride of place, especially if one examines the career of this particular farmer and the probable career of his son. The farmer has worked just as hard as his son will work and certainly for longer hours ; in addition he has had considerable capital at risk ; he has been assured of no salary whatsoever ; he has enjoyed no holidays by right but only those for which he could afford to pay ; and if he wants a pension in his old age it is up to him to provide for it. The son will do his job, risk no capital, receive an amount of salary fixed by law which will arrive for certain on the appointed day ; enjoy statutory holidays by right ; and a pension in his old age. The father will help to produce the income of the country ; the son will receive some of it in return for his services rendered.

I am old fashioned enough to suggest that we should always put first things first, and that for a farmer's son to become a salaried servant is a step down ; and, while I do not expect farmer fathers to agree with that valuation, nor blame them for trying to get their sons into safety first occupations, I do suggest that they might have a little more pride in their own calling and place it at least on a level with the salaried job.

*   *   *   *   *   *

Recently in almost every paper or magazine which I have perused I have found an appreciation or otherwise of the late Mr. Rudyard Kipling's work.

Some writers applaud his tales of India and the exploits of the immortal Mulvaney, Ortheris, and Learoyd. By others he is acclaimed as the master of the short story, as a writer for children, as a novelist, or as a poet, according to their taste. Some sneer at his imperialism, saying that his outlook never altered with the passing of time ; and occasionally he is decried as a snob. A few critics condemn his humour as being that of the little boy who says " Yah !" with delight at witnessing some unfortunate human being's discomfiture ; and many mourn him as a sincere lover of England and a magician with words.

But nowhere have I read anything which stresses the one phase of his work which appeals to me the most. I mean his stories and verses which deal with rural England and its inhabitants. To me, a farmer, his insight into the minds of countryfolk was uncanny. He never made a mistake. When he was writing about a farmer, he was himself a farmer ; when the need arose he became himself a farm labourer ; when he wrote of a wealthy American who settled in rural England, he, the writer became for the moment the American of his tale.

" A Habitation Enforced," which is, I think, the first story in the volume entitled, " Actions and Reactions," is to me the finest story of an English village that I know. " The Brushwood Boy " is perhaps a trifle on the snobby side, but it is a gracious love story which possesses the power to make the middle-aged reader enjoy his or her courtship once again. If you would recall the time when hunting first began to grip you, read " My Son's Wife." Would you laugh immoderately, try " My Sunday at Home", " The Village that voted the Earth was flat," or " Steam Tactics." If you would meet your friends amongst the farm labourers,

" Friendly Brook " will perform the introduction.   In every
reference to England's countryside the characters are so
right in every detail that one is forced to wonder just how
a man who spent so much of his early working life abroad
could have known them sufficiently intimately to be able
to depict them so faithfully.

The same uncanny knowledge of rural matters can be
found in Kipling's verses.   Here is a quotation from a poem
entitled " The Land," in which Kipling, as a landowner is
writing of the farm labourer :

"I have rights of chase and warren, as my dignity requires.
  I can fish—but Hobden tickles.   I can shoot—but
      Hobden wires.
  I repair, but he re-opens, certain gaps which, men allege,
  Have been used by every Hobden since a Hobden
      swapped a hedge.
  Shall I dog his morning progress o'er the track-betraying
      dew ?
  Demand his dinner-basket into which my pheasant flew ?
  Confiscate his evening faggot into which the conies ran,
  And summons him to judgment ?   I would sooner
      summons Pan."

I defy anyone to find the slightest suspicion of a mistake
in the above.

In these days of mechanized farming perhaps it would
not be out of place to refer to Kipling's power to invest a
machine with a soul, and yet not make it ridiculous.   " The
Ship that found herself " is perhaps the finest example, but
if anyone be captious enough to say that a ship is not a
machine let him read the story of " 267 " a racing locomo-
tive.   This power too can be found in Kipling's poetry for
in one instance he makes a Scotch engineer ask,

"Why don't poets tell ?
I'm sick of all their quirks and turns—the loves and doves
    they dream—
Lord, send a man like Robbie Burns to sing the Song o'
    Steam ! "

The foregoing definitely places me as a fervent admirer of Kipling's work. For some time now this has not been a popular role to fill, especially in the company of highbrows. But I am not and never will be ashamed of it. I have obtained more real joy and pleasure from reading Kipling than I have from the work of any other writer.

   *   *   *   *   *   *

In spite of the fact that I am continually stressing the financial importance of the poultry branch of our farming, I am not a poultry farmer to any extent. The trouble is that I dislike hens. Mentally we are not in sympathy, for I find it impossible to commune with hens in the same satisfying fashion as with other farm livestock. Also I am scared of them, and dread the risk of one panicking hen flying into my face when I open a stable door.

Of course, I am well aware that it is possible to avoid such frights by keeping hens in strict captivity under various forms of the intensive system, but that is such an inhuman business that as yet I have not attempted it. That it is efficient and profitable I know from the experience of my friends and neighbours, but while I can keep the wolf from the door without farming in such fashion I shall give it a miss.

However, no farmer should buy eggs—wait a bit, that needs qualifying. Let's try again. However, while a farmer will find it cheaper to buy eggs for his table unless his poultry farming be run on strictly ruthless and soulless lines, to do this looks bad in the eyes of the uninitiated. So my wife runs our small poultry department at my expense for her profit and both our pleasure.

Her stock (or should it be flock ?) are run on very old-fashioned lines, and in the poultry department we do everything wrong. I said as much to a neighbour who keeps some five thousand birds, and to my great astonishment he advised me to urge my wife to listen to no experts, and to continue so to do.

" Her way," he said, " she will get a few eggs and chicken worth eating with very little trouble or worry. 'Tother way she'll get more eggs and troubles galore. In fact, in a few years' time, unless we change our tune, the English fresh egg will be a devilish scarce article."

When I asked what he was getting at, he said, " We'm got too damn clever. We've bred our hens for enormous egg production. We feed 'em to boost it still higher. We hatch 'em artificially, and modern poultry farming has become so scientific and efficient that our hens now suffer from all the blame diseases imaginable. They die in thousands, and apparently there's no stopping 'em."

Thinking that he might be exaggerating I put a cautious note of his conversation into a farming paper, and the result was the receipt of letters from all over England in support of his opinions. Doubtless, modern poultry farmers will find a way to prevent his prophecy being fulfilled, but at the moment I'm sure that there's something not altogether happy in the poultry world. So my wife and her hens are carrying on according to ancient custom, and I continue to pay the bills and to eat eggs as is eggs and chicken which are worth eating.

*   *   *   *   *   *

The other day I heard a curious grouse against town life. A parson's son, who for his sins is compelled to live in London, told me that when he retired from business he intended to buy a house in the country which had plenty of barns and outhouses attached to it. The reason he gave was that in his present town house there was no room to put junk ; and that consequently his children were debarred from the joy of playing with the family relics.

Then he admitted that as a country rector's son he had had a much nicer upbringing than he had been able to provide for his own children.

" They're away at school." he said. " When they come home for the holidays our small town house becomes uncomfortably over-crowded. So we fire them off to a cottage in Devon or on a caravan holiday. As a result they never get any background, any roots ; and school, not home is their world. But as a kid I knew everybody in the village intimately no matter what their age, station, or calling. It's a valuable education for a child."

I'm not so sure that he didn't put his finger on one of the great drawbacks of a town upbringing as compared with a country one. Anyway, I hope he gets his outhouses before he is too old to enjoy filling them with all the junk which his wife now gives away.

*   *   *   *   *   *

One of my Wiltshire neighbours, who evidently considers that I am worth preserving a while longer, hearing that I had been down with " Flu," presented me with a bottle of mead. He also assured me that a glass of this liquid twice daily would soon put me right, and that he, a confirmed bee-keeper and mead-drinker, laughed at influenza and never even had a cold from one year's end to the other.

Of course, I took his advice, the whole blamed bottle of it, and either because of it or in spite of it I soon got better. Whether there is any medicinal quality in mead I know not, but there's the dickens of a kick to it. It is so luscious and so easy to drink that one does not realize its potency until after the second glass when one's legs tell the tale.

I don't think it is possible to buy mead to-day, although I suppose it is our oldest indigenous drink. The reason is probably because bee-keepers have been content to call mead by its old-fashioned name. But put it into champagne bottles, with wired-down corks covered with gold foil; call it Somebody's Wonderful Cocktail, Golden Beeswhisker; and I can imagine mead being sold in a London hotel at two shillings a wineglass. For no one can say that it would not compare very favourably with most modern cocktails either in taste or kick. Incidentally, if any bee-keeper makes a fortune out of this idea, I here put in a modest claim for five per cent.

*   *   *   *   *   *

Human nature being what it is, most folk feel much more content with their own lot when they hear of others who are obviously much worse off. I was forced to plead guilty to this failing after reading " Peasant Europe," by H. Hessell Tiltman.

It is a thick book, but it is by no means a dry one, while to any farmer it must be interesting reading. It deals with the state of the peasant peoples of Europe who live to the East of the frontiers of Germany, Switzerland, and Italy, or what the author terms " The other half of Europe."

Post-war international statesmanship altered many of the old boundaries, and forced many small nations into larger states. The result is that to-day a population of

100 million peasants are to be found in the following countries of Eastern Europe—Poland, Czechoslovakia, Austria, Hungary, Yugoslavia, Bulgaria, and Rumania.

The bulk of the population of these countries are peasants actively engaged in farming, and surely therefore as such they must warrant in some degree the interest of British farmers.   Contrast the figures in this country of only 7 per cent. engaged in agriculture—in Bulgaria 82 per cent., Poland 75 per cent., Rumania and Yugoslavia 80 per cent., Hungary 60 per cent., and 40 per cent. in Czechoslovakia.

In reading of their countries and of their lives, while I was sympathetic to those minorities who are now under an alien rule which is doing its utmost to destroy their old nationalism, I, as a farmer, was more interested in the condition of their industry and in their standard of living. Briefly they are in such a state of poverty that they are too poor to buy sufficient qualities of those three essentials of their village life—matches, salt, and oil.   Matches are definitely luxuries.   When a box of fifty safeties has been purchased it is so precious that a peasant, before using them —here I am quoting—" Splits each match into four, longways, so that a quarter of the head is left on each stick. Each box of matches thus becomes two hundred !   Thus are the peasant lands fighting the world depression."   In some cases they have gone back to flint and steel, but this in certain districts is an illegal practice, as matches are taxed.

Apparently taxing peasants is a popular game in these parts, for the author writes, " The value of a sheep in the Autumn of 1933 in Czernowitz market was 2s. 6d., while the amount charged before a peasant could take a sheep into the market for sale was 1s. 8d."   Somehow I don't think the most disgruntled dairy farmer can charge the Milk Marketing Board with quite such a rake-off.

Here is another note. " These peasants have little or no cash income. A census taken by the author in three hundred small farmsteads of Yugoslavia revealed that the *average* amount of actual money in the possession of these three hundred families amounted to 1s. per head."

Apparently they cannot sell their produce, and so they consume most of it. They feed their corn to their stock, and eat the result. They make their own clothes from their own produce, use candles made from sheep's tallow, and boots of sheepskin, which means that, " You will find almost every kind of disease and sickness in those primitive peasant houses—except malnutrition."

What about wages for farm employees ? " In 1932 the highest obtainable even in harvest times was 7d. a day for men and 5d. a day for women." This was in Rumanian Ukraine. Sometimes in desperation a small farmer will leave his holding. A tale is told of one such who tramped 200 miles on the chance of getting a month's harvest work in Yugoslavia at one shilling a day. " If I am lucky," he said, " I shall bring back enough cash to provide us with matches and salt for a year."

The author concludes with this statement, " If the day comes when the debt load is lightened, and the effective cash income of every peasant home raised to 5s. a week, Western Europe will discover that the potentialities of the vast Chinese market are no greater than the appetite of this ' other Europe ' which lies at our very doors."

Reading this book made me very conscious of the many blessings which I and other British farming folk, both masters and employees, now enjoy ; and also of the bitter competition which must come some day from these desperate folk in Eastern Europe. I will own that I am afraid of the future ; but, even so, I shall not emigrate to Eastern Europe yet awhile. Incidentally there is one saying of the European peasant, which farmers all over the world would do well to consider. " Whoever wins the next war the peasant will lose it."

*   *   *   *   *   *

This morning comes the news that the King is dead, or rather that the most beloved farmer in this island is now an honoured sheaf in the harvest of time.

It is not his show ring successes or his consistent anxiety for the well-being of our oldest industry which causes me to refer to his late Majesty in this fashion ; but rather because, whenever his duties permitted him to visit his Norfolk farms, he enjoyed his farming as an English country-man—a true Farmer George.

As a first-class shot and a courteous host at his large shooting parties his fame was world-wide ; but the shooting which he most enjoyed was very simple in character. One of his tenants told me only a year or so ago of a day's shooting when the late King, another tenant, and himself were the only guns, the total of their years being 210. His royal landlord asked him why he did not grow sugar beet, to which he replied, " Your Majesty, the partridges don't like 'em. What should we do wi'out a good piece o' turnips when we do have a nice quiet day together like this ?"

And now the King is dead, and his old tenant will shoot with his farmer friend no more. But, while the Norfolk farmers who knew him intimately will mourn the passing of a good landlord and a kindly neighbour, in every steading in this island those who serve the land will mourn the passing of a Royal Ruler ; who served it more faithfully than most, and who somehow or other possessed such majesty to make the lowliest peasant look upon him as a well-loved friend.

These few lines come aptly at the end of this chapter, for they mark the end of a chapter of England's history. In addition, they mark the beginning of a new one ; for now the father is dead, the son reigns in his stead. The English monarchy has a lot in common with English farming. Clever people criticize both ; disgruntled folk would have both cease in the interests of the mob ; and countless men and women all over the world wonder just why it is and how it is that both continue despite the manifold attacks of modernity. The continuity of such old-fashioned things is perhaps not logical in this world of change ; but here an illogical English farmer confesses—no, brags that he would not have it otherwise.

*   *   *   *   *   *

B . . . . the Weather

And anyone can translate the dots after the letter B just as it suits them, for my rendering is definitely not printable.

Never do I remember being so sick and tired of winter. I can remember much more snow and frost, quite as much rain, and just as long a winter, but never such beastly uncomfortable weather as the sample which has been dished out to us during the past three months. The wind keeps on harking back to the north-east; every other day it rains; and the result is that countryfolk can neither work nor play in comfort.

Hitherto I have always stuck up for the English climate, but now I am beginning to envy some of my overseas friends who are enjoying the sun. Here he is a wash out—a pale watery fellow, who has no warm friendliness in him. True, he rises at the proper time, and occasionally flushes the evening sky for a few moments, but that is all. I could forgive him for spoiling my pleasure—after all, neither hunting nor shooting require sunshine at this season, and a wetting while engaged in either is part of the sport—but I cannot help grousing at his refusal even to try to drive winter from the land. In consequence, work, farm work, is at a standstill. We mark time at the routine jobs connected with stock, but the land is such cold repellent stuff that men, horses, and machines are best away from it. Perhaps repellent is the wrong adjective, for in one sense the ploughland is anything but. It is wet and sticky, like cold porridge. Just now, anyone who is suffering from the old Liberal complaint of land hunger should walk across a field of fallows. He may not acquire a whole farm, but he will arrive at the far hedge with the beginnings of a nice small-holding on his boots.

Apropos of a wetting being all in the game for those who hunt, the conversation of two very good friends of mine the other afternoon is interesting. Both were countrymen, and both were golfers ; but while one was a farmer, the other had earned his living as a professional man in a small provincial town. They were talking business in the latter's office on the first floor, while the rain fairly pelted down outside. Hearing the clatter of horses, they went to the window and looked down into the gathering wet dark of the street, to see the South and West Wilts Hunt on its way home ; whereupon the farmer opened the window and leaned out in order to see if he could recognize any of the riders.

To him the sight recalled memories of the joys and sorrows of the many wettings he had experienced during his hunting days ; but to his friend it was merely an illustration of the imbecility of hunting folk.

" Look at them," he said, " Poor devils ! Wet to the skin, miserable as hell, and most of them with another hour's ride ahead. Fancy spending good money and putting up with that sort of discomfort just to ride across country after a bad smell ! They ought to be certified."

" Ever hunted yourself ?" asked his friend.

" Good gracious, no ! Give me credit for a bit of sense," came the reply.

" Then don't talk about something you ain't qualified to discuss. You don't know what you've missed. Don't

pity those chaps out there hackin' home in the rain, but
realize that they pity you, stuck up here in a stuffy office
with a blinkin' anthracite stove and musty papers for
company."

" Well, shut that window, and tell me what I've missed."

" Can't be done, old chap.   You wouldn't understand.
You may know a bit about your own job, but huntin's
beyond you.   And there's only one way to learn about it, and
that's to do it.   Gosh, I can remember years ago when I
had a good horse between my knees and hounds were
runnin' that I didn't care a damn what was 'tother side of
a fence nor if it snowed pink.   And I'd give a hundred quid
this minute to be able to do it again.   Come on, let's go to
tea and talk golf.   It's all we're both fit for now."

Which, although it was perhaps rather narrow minded,
expresses my sentiments to a nicety.   Golf and many other
games have and still do give me great pleasure ; but, when
I remember the lift of a horse over a fence, the wind in my
face, and the music of the pack, I realize just how poor they
are by comparison.

*   *   *   *   *   *

I've been reading the late Miss Winifred Holtby's book,
" South Riding."   Not only is it a good story, but it is one
of the most truthful pictures of English country life and
local government that I have ever come across.

Too often in modern fiction the countryman is unrecog-
nizable.   One school of writers depicts a loathsome,
illiterate, brutish fiend in human form ; while the other—
and here perhaps I must plead guilty—makes the countryman far too perfect a person in thought, word, and deed.
But "South Riding" gives a faithful picture of the Yorkshire
farmer.   His narrow-mindedness, his put-the-clock-back

attitude to all forms of social progress, his arrogance, his financial incompetence, and all his many other faults are there in good measure ; but, in addition, his virtues are shown in correct proportion. The Socialistic schoolmistress falls in love with him. Why, she cannot make out, for he stands for everything she loathes, and opposes her at every opportunity. The reason is, of course, that she is forced to recognize the quality in a man who from his birth had ridden straight. I know of no other book in which the author has been so fair to both ancient and modern in English country life.

* * * * * *

I heard a delightful story the other day, which illustrates that it is not always the best policy to put one's cards on the table. Some years ago a country gentleman invited an impecunious curate down to stay on the understanding that if he liked the look of his visitor he would give him a very good living which was in his gift. In his letter he informed his guest that there was a good trout stream, and that if he was a fisherman he should bring his rod.

Overjoyed the curate obeyed, and on his first day caught six brace of takeable trout. Result, he never got the living, and when a friend asked the reason, the Squire said, " What ? Make a fellow like that Rector ? Not likely ! Shouldn't have a damn fish in the river by Whit-Sunday."

* * * * * *

I know it is asking the impossible, but might I suggest that the press should publish something to inform the public that grass has a value to British farming. Most townsfolk don't know this, especially as they are continually fed with moans about the tragedy of laying land down to grass. Consequently, while they have some respect for other crops, they have none at all for grass.

A footpath at the side of an arable field remains a single footpath. But let the enterprising farmer invest some five pounds per acre in laying that field to grass and equipping it with fencing and water, and see what happens. That footpath will soon be twenty yards wide, and any request that people walk in single file as heretofore will be met with the bland remark, " But it's only grass."

So here, without fear of contradiction, I make the statement that GRASS is the most important crop in British farming, and that it is high time the town public were informed of this fact.

*   *   *   *   *   *

Presumably the B.B.C. is a national whipping boy, for the majority of people seem to criticize the wireless programmes most severely ; but here again I find myself on the side of the minority, for I am always amazed at their continued excellence. To produce a continuous programme for twelve hours daily from one year's end to another is no light task, and the responsibility of for ever finding something new must be nerve-wracking enough to send strong men into a lunatic asylum at the end of three months.

I was reminded of this the other afternoon when, after an Empire broadcast, I was summoned in council by two of the aforesaid strong men, who somehow manage to stand the strain and to keep sane. They had conceived the idea of a series of outside broadcasts under the title of " Night Shift," which would give listeners a little insight into the lives of some of their fellows who work by night. Did I think that a broadcast from a lambing pen would be not only possible but entertaining enough to begin the series ?

I replied that I thought it might be worth doing, whereupon the problem resolved itself into when and where. The first free date was towards the end of March ; and I left with instructions to find a farmer who had a flock which would be lambing in March, and who would be willing to let a broadcast take place in his lambing pen.

This job was not so easy as it sounds. For one thing most of the large arable flocks in my district lamb down in January or at latest February ; which meant that I should have to shoulder the displeasure of their owners by choosing a flock of grass sheep for the job. For another many grass flocks lamb down in the open, and I had to find a pukka lambing pen ; and to add to my difficulties the said pen had to be within a mile of a telephone exchange, in order that the connection from there to the site should not be so costly as to be prohibitive.

By great good luck one of my best friends and neighbours was able to fill the bill most admirably. His Exmoor ewes were due to begin lambing on March 25th, and the site chosen for the pen was within reasonable distance of the village post office. So I have reported progress, and the broadcast is now fixed for March 30th. My Hampshire Down friends are, as I thought, a trifle annoyed that mere Exmoors should be chosen for the job ; the owner of the chosen flock is most eager to help ; his shepherd makes no comment but thinks the more ; and I am wondering just what sort of mess the three of us will make of the job when the time comes.

* * * * * *

I spent this afternoon at the Farmers' Club, where I listened to Sir John Orr expounding his idea of marrying our agriculture and health policies. Few people, I think,

Country Pen. Winter

will disagree with the main principle involved—that the
purpose of production is consumption — and that it is
important ; for, when the underlying principle of a policy
is sound and right, no matter how difficult the task
appears, sooner or later mankind finds a way to achieve it.
It is when the principle is unsound that no clever plan can
succeed, no matter how expedient it appears to be to put
it into operation. Which, of course, is getting back to
those first principles which most of us learned at our
mother's knees. The longer one lives the more right they
become.

Briefly, Sir John's argument is this. Bad health in
a large section of our population is expensive to the nation.
Good health depends chiefly on proper nourishment. At
the moment we are leaving the question of nourishment
alone, and waiting until poor people are in such a state to
be candidates for medical attention. When this occurs, the
nation is willing to spend money on them, but not before.
Why not then spend some money on giving the under-
nourished proper food, and so prevent their bad health,
which means money spent in trying to put the wrong right ?
In other words he advises the nation to lock the stable door
on that good horse, Health, before the thief, Under-
nourishment, has stolen it.

He argues that the nation could buy good health by
means of a good food policy, and at the same time buy
a prosperous agricultural industry. To the critic who be-
moans the cost of such a Socialistic notion he points out
that we have already purchased sanitation, water-supplies,
education, and many other national needs, and that few
people can say that the expenditure involved has not been
a profitable national investment.

Surely then no town consumer of food can cavil at such a policy, except those who still nourish in their hearts an inherent hatred and mistrust of all farmers, the legacy of the hungry forties and the high prices for food during more recent war-time ? Unfortunately there are many such. They are in favour of all national spending on social services ; they would be willing to buy health as Sir John suggests ; but the very thought that such a policy might make the farmers of this country a trifle better off is enough to make them see red.

So many townsfolk to-day still look upon farmers as men who oppress their employees, and rob the consumer at every opportunity ; and as men who hunt two days a week, shoot two days a week, go to market two days a week, and sleep the sleep of repletion during most of Sunday. They have, and few politicians have, no conception of the change which has taken place in farming since the war ; and I doubt whether many of them will ever change their ideas about farming. Even so, I find it difficult to blame them for their attitude. How can they know what I and most farmers know ? That the gentleman farmer is practically extinct. That the tenant farmer who makes two thousand a year by swilling beer in markets never did exist, and very certainly does not exist to-day. That the whiners amongst farmers are becoming rapidly fewer, as hard times push out the inefficient. That the younger men who are going into farming to-day are going in on their feet with no false ideas of grandeur, but with a determined idea of wresting a fair living from the land of their own country by means of hard work and expert knowledge.

It is to these younger farmers that I hope Sir John Orr will plead his case ; which is merely an argument for production for consumption, for a fair living for the efficient producer only, and only then for the efficient producer of those " health " foods which our consumers most require. I meet these young farmers all over England. They have no false ideas about their business. They are not living in a world where barley made over a 100s. a quarter, milk 2s. 6d. a gallon, and other produce similarly inflated prices. They knew not such halcyon days, and therefore, having no hampering memories of affluence, they have no regrets—what an asset that is ! They are more than willing to invest their brains, their brawn, and their money in British land, as long as they can see a hope of a fair return. If the nation really wants a better health policy, which must be a good food policy, and therefore a good agricultural policy, the younger farmers of this country will try their utmost to make it a success ; and so will most of the older ones, for only those who are mentally young have been able to weather the financial storm of the past ten years.

Quite as bad as the town socialist who looks upon all farmers as profiteers is the dyed in the wool tory who moans aloud about pauperizing the masses. Presumably he or she—and how often it is a she—prefers to starve them. In support of their ideas such folk often quote the Scriptures, saying, " He that will not work neither shall he eat," or words to that effect. They forget that this statement was made at a time when he that would work could work, and so, as a result, eat his fill. That state of things does not obtain to-day. In spite of all the clap-trap which is talked of the thousands of unemployed who don't want work and who won't work, the fact remains that such folk are a very small minority indeed of the existing unemployed, and that there

are thousands of willing workers who cannot obtain work,
no matter how much they try. True, they receive unemployment pay, but Sir John Orr proves beyond contradiction
that this does not enable them to eat adequately.

Indeed, he proves much more to our shame—that not
only the unemployed are under-nourished, but that 50 per
cent. of our population are in like case, and that nearly
25 per cent. of our children are to be found in the lowest
income group, right down on the poverty line. I cannot
think that this wealthy nation will carry such a stigma much
longer ; and I have hopes, in spite of both rabid tories and
rabid socialists, that his sane ideas concerning agricultural
production and food consumption will be put into practice
in the not too distant future. What an infernal nuisance
the enthusiast is, to both friends and enemies !

*   *   *   *   *   *

One of my small-holder friends is a never-ending joy to
me. I do business with him to my great pleasure and to
both our profit—what greater compliment can I pay ? I
seek his advice concerning all sorts of things ; I value his
friendship ; and whenever I can do so I seek his company,
for his conversation has a quality which cannot be computed
in money, nor, I fear, set down in print. However, here
goes to try.

The other day he brought up the subject of the theatre.

" You do zee a lot o' play-actin' up in Lunnon, I 'low ? "
he said.

" No," I replied. " You see, I'm usually too busy when
I'm up there. Occasionally my wife and I go to a play in
town, but I never go alone. Shouldn't think I've been to
three in a twelvemonth."

" Aw ! " he said. " I zee. Young Mr. S— —, 'is

wife's a hactress. Jist about a pretty 'ooman, too. She wur beginnin' wi' a play down Bournemouth tother day, an' 'ee come to I wi' a ticket, an' asked I to goo down."

" And did you ?" I asked, thinking that to visit Bournemouth for such a reason would not have been sufficient attraction.

" Aw, yes. I went down. Thee's know. Volk in the same village. I couldn' do no less than goo down an' gi'e 'em a start."

Now, who says there is no such thing as village pride ? And how I regret that his subsequent sound criticism of the lady's performance was too pungent for publication !

*   *   *   *   *   *

Although farmers as a class are not supposed to keep accounts in these difficult times many of them do so, and the other day I was privileged to look at the accounts of numerous farms in Wessex. They were divided into four classes.

Class 1. Farms which were run by the farmer and his family, and on which little or no paid labour was employed—in other words, small-holdings, although according to the type of farming practised and the class of soil, the acreage varied from ten to one hundred and fifty acres.

Class 2. Farms of from two hundred to five hundred acres.

Class 3. Farms of from five hundred to one thousand acres.

Class 4. Farms larger than one thousand acres.

Now, strange as it may seem, Classes 1, 3, and 4, showed a profit while Class 2 showed a loss.

Further examination of the accounts showed all sorts of things, the chief of which was that the profitable farm is the one which uses the smallest amount of paid human labour per hundred pounds' worth of output. In obedience to this rule Class 1 did fairly well ; Class 3, the farms being large enough to make good use of mechanization, also did fairly well ; and Class 4, it's farms being large enough to make even better use of mechanization than those in Class 3, did very well indeed.

But Class 2 fell between the two stools of Classes 1 and 3. In almost every case the farms in it were not large enough to warrant an adequate mechanized equipment, nor to produce sufficient output to carry the human labour employed plus the upkeep of a large house, occupied in some cases by a non-working family. It was noticeable that the few farms in this class which did show a profit were all specializing on one or at most two products, and so were able to be mechanized up to the hilt.

This confirmed what I have long suspected from my own experience—that too often the mixed farm of from two to five hundred acres, although most politicians always refer to it as the backbone of British farming, is not a business proposition ; and that in a great many cases the farmer of it would be better off with either less land or more, usually the former.

What I mean is this—even where mechanization and specialization rule the farming it is very necessary to be farming at 125 per cent. of production rather than at 75 per cent. Let me take a hypothetical case by way of illustration.

A has a grass farm of two hundred acres, on which he can just manage to keep the economic unit of an outdoor

milking outfit and seventy cows. If A knows his job and
works he will do pretty well. B has a similar farm of 300
acres, on which he keeps the same sized outdoor herd. He
would like to keep one hundred cows, but such large herds
do not thrive well, and are difficult to manage in the short
winter days. So he keeps seventy cows, and sells some hay.
In nine cases out of ten B has a job to keep body and soul
together, and he would be much better off if he paid the
same rent for a hundred acres less.

Still, it is absurd for B or anyone to expect to find farms
cut exactly to the size to suit, so he must find a way out.
He may succeed by rearing young stock, or keeping pigs, or
even poultry on the extra acres ; but supposing milk production is his particular line and he wants to keep to it,
what then ? Then, he must stick to his last, and put on a
second herd of seventy cows. This will mean he will be
farming at 125 per cent of production, for to carry these
cows throughout the year he will be forced to purchase some
hay from another source and this will pay him very much
better than keeping half the number of cows and selling
some unwanted hay.

But, of course, to do this requires double the capital,
which so many farmers of B's type do not possess. Even
so, the longer I farm and talk to farmers the more convinced
I become that the only way to make money out of farming
is to use a farm as factory premises on which a considerable
amount of purchased raw material can be turned into
a readily saleable finished product.

*   *   *   *   *   *

February's over, thank goodness, for it has been a wet,
dirty, cold, and beastly uncomfortable month. I cannot
find anything bad enough to say for it. As a result the

farm work is all behind, and the countryside looks as barren in March as it did at Christmas.

In fact the only sign of better things is the behaviour of the birds. They seem to be getting on with their spring business in spite of the weather, a thing which the farmer cannot do. Let the sun shine ever so weakly for an hour or two, and the thrush sings gaily, while the sparrows are twittering on every roof. Most wild things seem to know that the shooting season is over, and that man is not now such a dangerous animal. In consequence they are quite cheeky. Only yesterday a woodcock flopped all round me, the easiest of shots. Catch him doing that a month ago. Then it would have been a swift zig-zag flight, bang bang, and the realization that I had missed, both barrels. As it was he took his time, and then dropped in a lazy slant into the hazel.

But if shooting is over, and farm work impossible, there still remains hunting yet awhile. I don't for one moment suggest that the fox enjoys being hunted, but here is a tale which shows that he is interested in the doings of the hounds. A few weeks ago our local pack met at a near-by village, and proceeded to draw a low long bank of covert which lies to the east of it. Report had it that this was a sure find, but Charles was not at home ; and it was not until a week or so later than I obtained the truth of the matter from a farm labourer.

" 'Ee wur there all right," he said, " although you didn' vind un. 'Ee wur sot out sunnin' 'isself in one o' they medders below 'ee. 'Ee watched 'ee draw down the ridge, and watched 'ee goo back. An' then the cheeky varmint gets up and follers 'ee dainty an' quiet like jist to see wot wur gwaine on."

Walhut 'ee down in ridge

" How the dickens do you know ?" I asked.

" Cause I wur up top a hayrick an' zeed it all. An' I 'ollered, but the wind wur agen I, zo you didn' hear me," came the reply.

How that fox must have enjoyed himself !

*   *   *   *   *   *

Hounds met on my lawn last Saturday, and in spite of a cold drizzle they made a pretty picture. After a swiftish drink we set out for Grovely. I must confess that I was rather glad it was Grovely that day, for in order to get home —and my small daughter would have expired if I had not done so—I was obliged to drive down from London late on Friday night, arriving in the small hours of Saturday morning. In consequence I was on the sleepy side.

Perhaps here I should explain that Grovely is a wood seven miles long by about a mile and a half wide. Usually we cannot get a fox out of it, but just go round and round rather gently along lovely squishy rides between the nut-bushes. This, I decided, would just about suit my mental and physical condition.

But in March anything can happen, for foxes will move in March. There was a thick mist with rain, and for some time hounds could find nothing. At last we did find, and had half-an-hour's usual woodland hunting according to schedule. Then, suddenly, we were away out on the downs on the north side, and going like smoke. " He's for Stonehenge." yelled the huntsman, and it looked like it. Apparently Charles had decided to cross the flooded Wylye river, and lose us on Salisbury Plain beyond. But just as he got to the railway, a train came by, and to cap matters whistled loud and shrill. Result, we were soon back in Grovely once more, and there we stayed until we lost all trace of our fox.

By this time it was three o'clock, and as we were all wet through we decided to call it a day.

And on Sunday morning my horse was lame, which puts paid to any more hunting for at least a week. That's the worst of pulling down 15 stone. Still, if spring would come along I shan't mind, for I want to get on with all sorts of work on the farm. It's all very well to say that a farmer must have a goodly supply of faith and patience. My store of both is running very low.

Incidentally, shepherds and huntsmen have one thing in common. It is amazing how both know the idiosyncrasies of every one of the animals under their charge. A shepherd will tell you the private history of any sheep you care to point out ; and last Saturday I noticed that our local huntsman knew the habits of one of his hounds to a nicety.

When we decided to call it a day we were one hound short. " Ah, that'll be Derby. No good to blow for him," said the huntsman to the Master. " A German band wouldn't fetch him home. He'll roll back when he's ready."

At eight p.m. that evening the local grocer rang me up to say that Derby was in his shop, and refused to leave, although they had fed him with biscuits. Derby is evidently a hound of parts. He knows a good biscuit when he gets it.

*   *   *   *   *   *

Of course, there's some farm work which goes on in spite of the weather. Lambs are bleating on many Wiltshire hillsides, and, though their mothers haven't had a dry back since October, the luck generally is pretty good. I don't keep any sheep now, but I had this on the authority of one of my shepherd friends in the Salisbury district. Indeed, I had more, for he brought me some lamb tails as a present.

This delicacy, I believe, is one of the few things in these days which cannot be purchased for money. The lamb tails belong by right to the head shepherd, and only through his courtesy can a sufficiency of them be obtained to make a lamb tail pie. My wife tells me that they are an awful trouble to prepare, but the result would seem to justify it. In fact, there is only one drawback to lamb tail pie—it is so tasty that one is tempted to eat with gusto, and so rich that in many cases this is followed by internal regrets.

Which reminds me that our lambing pen broadcast is due in a few weeks' time, and that I must soon get busy about it.

*   *   *   *   *   *

I suppose that to write newspaper headlines of the necessary startling sort one must have a special type of mentality which is suited to this calling. Or is a long apprenticeship essential? Anyway, I feel certain that foreigners must be often mislead by the result.

An uninitiated reader, seeing the headline, " Serious blow to England," will naturally expect to read of the death of one of her famous men, of the collapse of one of her greatest industries, or of some similarly important national disaster. It is to be imagined, therefore, when he discovers that the headline refers to the fact that an English cricketer has sprained his thumb, that he is a trifle disappointed and perhaps puzzled.

I must confess that I have at times been startled by headlines like " Gilts falling sharply " or " Gilts a trifle easier ". For a moment I have thought either of the Gadarene swine or of how nice it was that the paper was so concerned for our pigs' welfare ; only to find later that the headline referred to the movements of gilt-edged stocks and shares—things which I have never possessed. Consequently, I have formed the habit of disregarding newspaper headlines as of no importance, in that they were misleading ; which is, for their writers, yet another instance of desire outrunning performance.

But the other Sunday I came across a truly agricultural headline, which did refer to the reading matter beneath. Even so—being, I fear, of a naturally sarcastic disposition— I cannot help criticizing the tone of both the headline and the article beneath it. With the main headline I have no quarrel. " Vegetable Famine in Britain " seems a fair way to describe the present shortage of green vegetables. But the sub-title read, " People buying sheep fodder."

Apparently, according to the writer, there is something awful in this happening. But why ? Since when have cabbages, and kale, and turnips, and swedes, been other than sheep fodder? That human beings also eat them merely shows either their intelligence or that of sheep— I cannot make up my mind just which. Later on the writer lamented that people in the lower income groups had to put up with rape greens or turnip tops. Most rural folk have not *put up* with these delicacies throughout their lives in early spring ; they have been glad of the chance to enjoy such a succulent dish.

Still, in case any newspaper man is running out of ideas, I here suggest to him the headline, " Deplorable state of England. People eating bread made from poultry food." And if he wishes to turn from food to drink. " Poor people only able to drink beer made from hog's food." From these he can run the gamut of most of the crops of British farming.

During the past week I have been nearer to buying a farm than ever before in my life. Not that I can afford to do such a thing, but because, just when I was feeling rather disgruntled with my present one, I had the offer of something which seemed very attractive.

The disgruntled feeling was due to several causes—the after effects of a bout of influenza ; general depression owing to weather ; the rapid surrounding of my house with council houses, and now the news that a town water main is to be run through a forty acre pasture during April, May and June, when that pasture should be laid up for hay ; and a general feeling that to farm three hundred and twenty acres properly and to tramp the writer's treadmill in similar fashion was getting beyond my capabilities. It seemed that the only remedy for all these worries must be a smaller farm with a smaller house, situated in some very rural village where borough surveyors would cease from troubling and a weary countryman might find rest.

The desire for a smaller house is, I think, sound ; and so is the wish to live further away from modern progress. Indeed, rural privacy and peace will undoubtedly become more sought after and more expensive in consequence as the years go on. Already the day is gone when the house on a main road and near a station is for that reason more desirable ; and the same might truthfully be said concerning farms. Modern road transport has materially discounted these one-time advantages in two ways. Firstly, by bringing the farm which is ten miles from market or station only twenty minutes away ; and secondly, by the lack of privacy and control which proximity to town now entails. But the desire for a farm small enough to be no worry and only a play-game is, I know, a foolish one, even while it may be understandable. If there be any merit at all in my scribbling, it is because I am a farmer ; because farming problems are of necessity my problems, because the vagaries of our climate do materially affect my pocket, and because, instead of writing about farming from outside in, I cannot help doing it from inside out. Consequently, I realize that I should be worse than a fool cowardly to run away from this whip of circumstance which manages to keep me straight at my fences.

But recently the desire to be able to turn my head at the lowest of jumps if I felt so inclined has seemed very tempting, and this farm which I was offered had so many things to recommend it. It was half the size of my present farm ; there was not one bad acre on it ; the price, if not exactly cheap, was certainly not dear ; there were some trout in the stream at one end, and some twenty pheasants in a copse at the other ; and to cap all it boasted an old Tudor farmhouse of stone and thatch.

This last was excellent, for my wife had always said firmly that she would not move, unless it was to a really old house of character, so I took her down to inspect the place. Alas ! It was too old, the rooms were too low and gloomy, the thatched roof needed costly repair, and she said that she would be afraid to go to bed at night in such a medieval castle. In fact, the house had too much character for her. Next time I shall suggest a modern bungalow.

Another thing which influenced my wife against the place was that it was not situated in a proper village which had a church and a pub and a village hall, but in a small hamlet which boasted none of these necessary features of rural life. And in this I was on her side. It was the lack of a church which seemed the greatest drawback. You may be a good churchman or a bad one, a Nonconformist, a Roman Catholic, a Mohammedan, or an Atheist ; but in either case, if you wish to live in an English village, you will prefer one which has a proper church as a kind of rallying point for the other buildings and communal activities.   Even in these days, when its influence in rural districts is becoming rapidly weaker, the Church of England still stands for that.

However, I still hankered after the place, whereupon my wife said firmly, " Well, buy it if you want to, but you'll have to get another woman to go there with you, for I shan't."

That, of course, was a bluff which I dared not call, even though the old Adam in me urged me so to do ; and, very regretfully, I abandoned the idea of purchase.   But I still find it interesting to wonder whether I could have found that other woman to share my medieval castle, and also what my wife's reactions would have been to such a happening.

    *   *   *   *   *   *

For some time now I have noticed that the countryman loathes thatch with the same intensity with which the townsman loves it ;   and this afternoon, when I was telling a neighbour of my thwarted ambitions to become a land-owner, I obtained further confirmation of this difference of opinion.

" That place !" he said, when I told him of my Naboth's vineyard.   " You let that alone.   You'd have to eat your midday meal by artificial light during winter ;   and it's so damn gloomy that you'd write nothing but tragedies if you lived there.   Besides you must be mad to consider it. It's thatch."

" Well, what of it ?   Thatch can be repaired," I retorted.

" Oh ah, if you'm a blinkin' Rothschild. But thatch means drip, drip, drip, every wet day. Drive a man to drink in a week. I've lived in a thatched house and I know."

Next to the expense of its upkeep this drip business is the greatest drawback to thatch as the roofing material for one's house. It is possible, I know to put some form of guttering to a thatched roof ; but, while this stops the drip, it destroys all the charm and beauty of the thatch. Anyone who is thinking of buying a thatched house should inspect it on a pouring wet day during winter ; for on a sunny summer day every thatched house looks so charming that the possibilities of drip are forgotten.

Another thing which influences many townsfolk in their choice of a country home for their retirement is its address. One man I knew told me that he would willingly pay an extra hundred pounds in order to live in Wallop. " Think of getting one's letters addressed to The Willows, Wallop, Hants !" he said. " Why it would be dirt cheap at a hundred quid. Reading the envelopes at breakfast time would be as satisfying as bacon and eggs. Wallop ! You can almost taste a nice fat rasher as you say it."

Most folk, I think, would prefer rashers without Wallop to Wallop without rashers, but I will confess that the two together are irresistible. Indeed, part of the attraction of the place which I so nearly bought lay, I think, in the fact that it was a Manor House ; and that had I bought that farm my address would have been ———— ——Manor. For I rather fancy myself, if not as Lord of a Manor, as occupier of one ; there being just as much snob in me as in most of us.

*   *   *   *   *   *

How true it is that farmers must always realize that the

well-being of their business is in the hands of a power greater than mankind ! Which means that they must have not only patience but also faith, that faith without which all man-made farming equipment is useless.

This year, even where the old faith remains, the supply of patience is running out. How much longer must we wait for spring is the prevailing cry ? Farmers shrugged their shoulders at January's floods, and looked to February for better things. But this month failed them. Spring never even flirted with us for a few days as is her custom, and February wept copious tears at such a jilting. And now, here is March, and winter's standstill order still remains in force.

Some few impatient spirits are already rebelling. In cold wet land of the consistency of porridge they are sowing oats. Sowing ? No, mudding them in for want of patience. Of what use your work, oh ye of little faith ? The soil is too cold for the seed to germinate quickly, and while it lies in its wet, uncomfortable bed the rooks will take their toll. And what pleasure was there in such work ? None at all, for at every step across the uninspired land it was borne in on the farmer, his men, and even his straining horses and labouring tractor, that they were doing wrong.

Better far to wait for spring and a proper seed-bed ; for that she will come there is no question. To-day is cold, with a sleety drizzle coming from the north-east, but to-morrow even may see spring with us once again—come not for a fleeting visit but to stay, and to cheer up man and bird and beast and plant and tree with her glad promises.

One fine morning we shall wake to find the wind in the west, and spring laughing wherever we walk. Then, in such a short time, the countryside will wake up to laugh with her. Suddenly it will be shirtsleeve weather. Then, work will be a pleasure, for the land will have lost its cold unfriendliness, and feel alive and companionable under one's boot. On the arable, now no longer horrible, there will be warm dust ; and on the pastures a tiny new-born clover leaf will brave one's boot at every step. Then, anyone who passes through the lovely pageant of England's countryside will see what spring means to the farmer— permission to do good work at full speed under favourable conditions. What a hurry the countryside will be in ! Tractors snorting and fussing over the fields ; horses plodding patiently and steadfastly up and down them ; allotments and gardens clicking like a hive of bees ; and even the birds house-building against time. This pleasant bustle on the hills and in the valleys will not be work per- formed sullenly in obedience to that stern tyrant, winter ; but rather service given eagerly in response to the gay encouragement of that laughing mistress, spring.

We cannot farm without her. We cannot speed her coming. Come she must and come she will, but in God's good time. We must wait her pleasure in faith and patience. But it is only human to implore her to hurry, for this season, owing to her tardiness, the farm work is all behind.

In spring when woods are getting green,
I'll try and tell you what I mean.

A Weeping Maiden

I do not know what the official date of spring's coming should be, but to-day, March 10th to be exact, is the first day for months when the breeze on the hills has been minus its winter bite. The sun is shining, the birds are singing, and at long last spring has come to cheer a winter-worn countryside.

In consequence, every farm hereabouts is showing signs of activity. On the hills the oats are going in. In the pastures the chain harrow is making lovely alternative light and dark green streaks from end to end ; just the same effect as brushing velvet first the right way and then the wrong. And down in the water meadows the drowner is shutting out the water, in the hope of drying the land ready for the cows. Spring is late this year, but now she has come I hope that it is to stay. If so she will make the whole countryside wake up and bustle, for what a lot of work there is which is crying out to be done !

Still, in spite of a long uncomfortable winter, farming has not come through too badly. The stock are in good flight, the hay is lasting out, and only the wheat plants seems to have suffered to any appreciable extent from the continued wet. Gosh ! If the weather were the only thing which farming had to fight, what a lovely game it would be !

*   *   *   *   *   *

Great grief at home to-day. I had promised to take Pam to the South and West Wilts Point-to-point at Deverill, but this morning she woke up covered with spots. These

were immediately diagnosed as German measles, so Pam
was definitely a non-starter. Which, of course, meant that
her mother followed suit ; and this decided me to work
rather than to play. So I stayed at home with the desk
well tucked into my tummy, and managed to write another
chapter of a novel.

This book is worrying me tremendously. I started it
lightheartedly before Christmas ; but the further I get
with it the more difficult the job seems to be. Three times
have I scrapped everything and started again, and even now
I am not at all sure that the pattern is the right one for the
theme. Still, to-day's chapter pleased me. It even made me
laugh aloud when I read it through. Whether that is a good
sign or not, I do not know ; but I am hoping that some of
my critics will have a similar sense of humour to mine.

* * * * * *

I must confess that I am not in the best of tempers,
although I am afraid that the reason is largely my own
fault, in that my previous remarks on the lateness of Spring's
coming must have upset that young lady. She is here at
last ; she has dressed the countryside in a lovely lush green,
the green of England's grass; but she is so very teary. Day
and night she weeps incessantly, and there is no sunshine
to comfort her.

Anyway, for some reason or other she has come without
her customary supply of face powder, for that March dust—
usually priced at a guinea a bushel—I have not once seen
her use. True, with or without this aid to beauty I love
her, and I admire her green frock tremendously, but I do
wish she would hurry up and powder her nose.

No farmer can be lyrical about weather conditions
for very long. What I really mean is that spring's recent

Mr Freeman in the Cynical stance. Weather conditions very Cong

habits suit neither my farming, my pocket, nor my temper.
I have grass all over my farm, but the irony of it is that I
cannot feed it to my cows. My water-meadows are living up
to their name—a large portion of them being literally under
water ; my pastures are too soft to carry the cattle ; and
so, with grass to spare, I am compelled to continue feeding
my dairy herd on hay and cake.

So much for dairying. The arable farming is in even
worse case. I have a field of oats half sown, and goodness
knows when we shall be able to get on it again, for the fallows
are like porridge. Which reminds me of a conversation I
had with a townsman the other day. He chided me and all
British farmers for being so individualistic, so unbusiness-
like, and so unwilling to co-operate with our neighbours.
Thinking of my experience that my neighbours were always
eager to give a helping hand wherever possible, I demanded
specific examples of our incompetence. Whereupon he
suggested that it was idiocy for each farmer to have a drill,
a tractor, a broadcast, and various other implements. Such
duplication was bad business, he argued. One tractor or
one drill could do the work of several farms.

The rain was peppering the windows as he spoke, so I
just told him.

" You are quite right," I said. " For the past few days
my tractor has not moved a yard. Neither have my drags
and harrows. I could have lent them to anyone for a whole
week without affecting my own farming in the slightest.
And during that time I could have borrowed cultivating
and sowing tackle from any of my neighbours quite as
easily."

" Then you agree," he began.

" No, I disagree entirely. Look here, during that week

there wasn't a drill in Wiltshire that stirred a foot. The weather wouldn't permit. But give us three dry days, and you wouldn't be able to hire one for love or money. That's the trouble with farming—every farmer wants to use the same implement at the same time. I grant you that we might do a trifle more in the way of co-operation, and even in sharing implements; but the essential implements every farmer must have of his own, so that he has the sole right over them when the weather permits their use."

Funny how everybody assumes the right to tell farmers how to run their business. Few farmers are arrogant enough to tell the average townsman how to run his.

* * * * * *

I was up on a Wiltshire down this afternoon, and I could not help noticing that the increasing fashion of keeping cattle out on the downs throughout the winter does much to reduce their rabbit population. I don't mean that out-door cattle chase and kill rabbits, but that their continual wandering over the downs disturbs the burrows.

Rabbits don't like being disturbed, and a cow's foot coming through into one's living room or passage must be distinctly disturbing. Anyway, on this down many of the burrows were so trodden in that I doubt whether they will be re-opened this summer to anything like the extent they were last year.

And possibly this continuous wet will shrink the rabbits too; for very certainly it was the three dry years which brought about such an increase in these vermin. But I hope 1936 is not going to try to emulate 1879 in the matter of wet weather. Recently I have been reading about that disastrous year, and it was not pleasant reading. Apparently, as a result of '79's wet, liver fluke in sheep—what one of my neighbours calls " coathed "—was so bad that at fairs one sheep in every lot was killed, and the liver exposed on the hurdles of the pen, in order that intending purchasers could judge the condition of the remainder.

Incidentally, if anyone can tell me the derivation of the word " coathed " I shall be greatly obliged.

*   *   *   *   *   *

Spring has brought many other colours to the country-side in addition to the green of grass. Just now the woods are showing all shades. These are due, not to any leaves being out, but to the differing colours of the swelling buds. The massed effect is very lovely. To see it properly you want to get some distance away on a hill, so that you can look down on a coppice : for when you get right in a wood, you are practically back in winter once more. The carpet beneath your feet is brown with last year's leaves ; the ground is wet and squelchy as it was in December ; and only the paper-white trunks of the birches relieve the winter gloom.

*   *   *   *   *   *

Usually a doctor is not exactly a welcome visitor to any home, but a few days ago our local medico made himself very popular with Pam and me. The measles had run their course, but he suggested that it would be sound policy for the convalescent not to return to school again this term. Naturally Pam was overjoyed at the thought of being able to ride daily ; and I was just as pleased because this means that I shall get my companion back again.

So yesterday, by way of celebration, we went hunting. Alas ! A sharp rain storm forced me to bring Pam home early, for the powers that be had warned me that to get wet through was not the best thing for recent " measley " patients. Which was a pity, for it cleared up in the after-noon, and they had a good run. However, by way of consolation I promised Pam that she should ride my big horse, Peter, on the morrow.

And this morning she did it, while I rode her fat cob. Peter behaved like the gentleman he is, but Thomas Webster found my weight much too steadying an influence. Pam managed Peter so well, that when she asked me if she could really let him go I had not the heart to refuse. So I told her to wait behind with him until Tommy had struggled with me half way up a long downland slope, and to let him go when I signalled.

It all happened according to plan, and the old gentleman flashed past Tommy and me at full gallop. If there is any prettier sight than a laughing eager little girl on the back of a thoroughbred stretched out like a Derby winner, I have yet to see it. For a moment I wondered whether she would be able to stop him, but he knew the value of his cargo, and came to hand like a lamb. It occurs to me that this morn-ing's performance may mean that father has lost his horse.

*　*　*　*　*　*

The lambing pen broadcast is timed for ten p.m., so this evening and yesterday evening I have been down to the sheepfold in order to try to catch the mood of the scene. Yesterday it was fine, and this evening was wet ; so, having a taste of both flavours, I shall be prepared for whatever type of weather spring dishes up on the night.

What a lot one can see out of doors even on the darkest night ! When I first left my car this evening, and stumbled across the field toward the lambing pen, I could not see a thing, not evening my feet ; and when I almost trod on a partridge, which exploded like a rocket under my toes, I shied like a startled horse. But after a few minutes I found that it was not really dark at all. There is a world of difference between being in the dark indoors and out. In the former case one feels smothered in black crepe ; in the latter one is caressed in cool grey velvet.

I must say that I have enjoyed these two lonely visits to the lambing pen, but I am wondering whether microphones and wireless engineers and control motor vans will not rather spoil the feel of the night. Alone I soon felt in tune with my surroundings. The outline of the downs against the night sky, showed me their lovely swoops and curves. I heard the sharp bark of a hunting fox, the screech of an owl, and only when a car buzzed along the road was I reminded that so many of us have sold our birthright for a mess of machinery.

And somehow, being alone in the countryside at night-time, although it does make one feel rather small, it does send one home to bed feeling extraordinarily pleased with life.

    *   *   *   *   *   *

To-day it was fine, and as the hounds were meeting within three miles of us Pam and I took a day off. The sun shone ; all the flies in the world hatched out and got busy on both riders and horses ; everybody was cheerful ; and we not only found a fox but he passed within twenty yards of Pam and me to her great delight. But we did not get a run for there was no scent whatsoever. The why and wherefore of scent or lack of it are apparently "wropt in mystery" even in these enlightened and scientific days ; which is, I think, one of the attractions of hunting. Life in other directions has become much too much a business of pushing the button and the figure moves. Indeed, sometimes I

think that man has arrived at the point when he thinks
that there is no God but man, and what a clever devil he is.
What is the quotation ? " Whom the gods would destroy
they first make mad," or words to that effect. Well
there is no doubt in my mind that countryfolk, even those
horrible folk who hunt, will remain sane longer than townsfolk ; for in their daily lives they are continually forced to
admit the existence of a Higher Power than themselves.

*   *   *   *   *   *

In a vain attempt to get my mind away from my respon-
sibilities concerning to-morrow's broadcast I have been
thinking about a unique feature of our national life—that
alone amongst industrial peoples we seem to have come to
terms with the countryside. What I mean is that in
England, one of the most thickly-populated and most highly
industrialized countries in the world, there is more wild life
to be seen than in any other of similar character. In the
field immediately touching the town, within a hundred
yards of houses and factories, there is always a pair of
partridges living and mating undisturbed by man's noisy,
busy life near by. The hare sits in her form, or dances a
grave minuet with her fellows, never heeding the cars and
buses which rush by in full view. The fox barks on the
hillside at the back of every town. Wild duck, moorhens,
kingfishers, and other water fowl swim and dive and nest
on the busiest river. On many roads the pheasant cocks
up to roost almost directly above the stream of glaringly-lit
traffic.   The rabbit nibbles demurely and completely ignores
man, until man deliberately forces himself upon its notice ;
while pigeons, thrushes, wrens, and hundreds of other birds
live their lives in happy content almost in the midst of man's
daily bustle.

more wild beasts and birds than any other country

To me this is both astounding and wholly delightful. Here in England, midst a nation famed beyond all others for its delight in hunting and killing wild beasts and birds, there are more wild beasts and birds than in any other country of comparable industrialism and density of population. Anyone who uses his eyes in the countryside will be forced to notice this strange but charming phenomenon ; and perhaps to wonder whether the credit for it should not be given to our national liking for blood sports. It is yet another example of the English flair for achieving the right result by a hopelessly illogical method. Anyway, whatever be the reason, there is no doubt that we have learned how to come to terms with the countryside better than any other nation in the world.

*   *   *   *   *   *

An outside broadcast always means much more work per minute of actual production than does the ordinary studio business. Indeed, in connection with this lambing pen job one labourer can say that he was worthy of his hire. Two journeys to London ; considerable motoring and telephoning in order to find a suitable flock and willing owner ; two nights on the ground gathering material ; writing two possible lay-outs of the show ; and all day yesterday preparing and finally broadcasting at ten p.m. I do not know what such an outside broadcast cost per minute, but it must have been an expensive job ; for there were many other folk employed in producing only a fifteen minute show, while the Post Office charges must have been considerable.

After lunch, I drove the B.B.C. producer down to the scene of action. There we found Post Office engineers, B.B.C. ditto, the farmer, the shepherd, and some two hundred and fifty Exmoor ewes, together with a few early lambs. How true it is that most folk always find the other fellow's job more interesting than their own ! The shepherd and his helpers were far more interested in microphones, amplifiers, and other strange gadgets, than they were in the sheep ; while the engineers were so fascinated with the natural processes which were going on all around them that they seemed almost bored with their own marvellous equipment. They knew all about moving coils and travelling " mikes," but when a lamb suddenly arrived almost under their feet they were absolutely flabbergasted. And, when the new arrivals got up and took their first drink in this world a few minutes afterwards, one of the engineers admitted to me that the whole business was far more interesting than everything in Broadcasting House added together.

When the " mikes " were in position we attempted some sort of a rehearsal, only to learn, as one always learns, that it is useless to prepare an outside broadcast beforehand. We altered the script, and we rehearsed our alterations, but the result was hopeless. True, the sheep baaed and bleated beautifully, but we could not get a word out of the shepherd impromptu, and he informed us that he could not see well enough to read from a typescript. The farmer confided to me that this was the first he had heard of Hubert's—everybody called him, Hube—poor sight, but there it was. Hube stuck his toes in, and refused to budge.

By eight p.m. we were in despair. We had nothing which would tell a story, or give the listener any impression of the actual scene. " It's bad," said the producer, " very bad, but if we can't think of anything better, it'll have to go as it lies. Can you suggest anything ?"

As a last resort I suggested that we were making a mistake in treating me as an experienced broadcaster who had come down from London to give an expert running commentary on night work in a lambing pen.

" Down here," I said, " I'm not a broadcaster. I'm a farmer. The owner of this flock has known me from boyhood. I'm his neighbour. Both he and the shepherd look upon me as a personal friend. If they were both ill to-night I could do their job, and lamb down these ewes. Why not let me blunder into the shepherd's house, ask them what sort of luck they're having, and chance what happens ? They'll talk to me."

The producer agreed, and so did the farmer, who was as worried as we were. In order to restore our shattered nerves he invited us back to his house for a quick one. Never has a drink seemed more golden, and thus fortified we went back to do or die.

So at ten o'clock we chanced the business on actuality, and the shepherd was the star of the show. After describing the night scene for a minute or so, I ran across to the shepherd's hut, opened the door, and said to the farmer, " Hullo, Jack ! How goes it ?" And from that moment it went with a swing. The thing which unlocked Hube's heart underneath his corduroy waistcoat was when I asked him whether the local hounds, which had met near by that day, had had any luck, for I knew that he had lost some lambs through foxes last year.

" Ketched a couple," he said with satisfaction. " Main good job, too. Ther' be too many o' they divils about."

And in a lovely deep bass voice, when he was due to leave the shepherd's hut to go round the lambing pen, he said, " I maun jist make up thease yer vire," which he proceeded to do with much clattering and a complete absence of nervousness. And when, while going round the lambing pen, he referred to one particular ewe as " A zhirkin' wold zod " I gave thanks for the capacity of the true countryman to rise to any occasion.

In fact, there was only one performer who did not do definitely better during the actual broadcast, than during rehearsal. This was an orphan lamb, which the shepherd was bottle-feeding in the shepherd's hut. During every try-out during the afternoon, he or she—I never discovered which—bleated like a good un. But during the show we got never a squeak.

*   *   *   *   *   *

The most popular comment on the lambing pen job is for my friends, either in town or country, to tell me that " the sheep were excellent "; which undoubtedly they were. Still, I think that the broadcast was justified, if only to show many listeners that there is still one branch of farming which has not yet been mechanized, and which is carried on in much the same fashion as it was in biblical days.

There was one curious thing about the setting of that show—the sheep were on the actual site of Fovant camp, and eighteen years before the ground on which the lambing pen stood was covered with army huts, which were occupied by German prisoners. Wiltshire may not have beaten her swords into ploughshares, but she has replaced army huts and German prisoners with a lambing pen and sheep and lambs. When I was standing by the microphone in that peaceful simple setting I could not help thinking of this change, and also that no one could deny that it was a change for the better. Does anyone want to see the sheep and lambs disappear, and the army huts return to Fovant's fields ?   Surely not !   The quiet beauty and wholesomeness of the present use of those acres of England— surely that is the better part ?   May it never be taken away from us.

*   *   *   *   *   *

I finished up that broadcast by saying something to the effect that soon the farmer, the engineers, and myself would be fast asleep in bed, but that the shepherd would keep his lonely vigil until the dawn.   Of course, this was meat to some of my more ribald friends, who have had great fun teasing me that instead of going back to bed I had gone back to my friend's farmhouse to carouse, apparently also until the dawn.

That is as it may be, but some information has just come to hand which puts the joke on some of the jokers.   On hearing my final remarks the wife of one of them said to her husband, " Catch Arthur going back to bed yet awhile. He and Jack'll be celebrating."   Her husband suggested that no matter what giddy escapades we might indulge in it was high time that he and his wife went to bed.   Promising to switch out the light outside their front door the lady agreed, and this done they went to bed.

Next morning the dairyman said to her husband, " What's lave thic outside light burnin' vor all night ?" Result, all square, my friends.

*   *   *   *   *   *

Just one more reference to sheep, and still another about rain.   The owner of the flock used in the broadcast told me that one wet night some years ago, he walked up to his lambing pen in the middle of the night.

" Thought I'd come up to give you a hand, shep., as 'tis

rainin' cats and dogs," was his greeting. To which the shepherd replied, " An' I be main glad to zee 'ee, zur. For tain't on'y rainin' cats an' dogs up yer, 'tis rainin' lambs."

Funny how rough weather always seems to bring on birth with farm livestock.

       *   *   *   *   *   *

But no matter what the weather, we south country farmers should be a deal more thankful for our many blessings than we are. This has been borne in upon me from reading Margaret Mary Leigh's book, " Highland Homespun." The chapter titles, " Making hay while the sun does not shine," and " Harvesting in the deluge," speak for themselves ; while the description of first putting hay and corn on to a wire fence, and then on an indoor rack, in order to get it sufficiently dry to stack, told me something of what the Highland farmer has to face with regard to weather. Indeed, I could have done with more harvesting operations and fewer bulling cows ; which, to my mind, take up far too many pages. It is queer what a fascination the latter sort of happening has for so many people. But that is my only criticism.

I understand that the author has abandoned the struggle in the north, and is now farming in the south-west of England. I should imagine that she finds the contrast between her present setting and her previous one very pleasant ; but I am glad that she stayed in the Highlands long enough to give us such a charming and realistic picture of life on Achinabo Farm.

       *   *   *   *   *   *

In a weak moment I have promised to write a chapter in a book which is being published with the idea of drawing attention to the destruction and spoiling of our rapidly

On a Highland Farm

shrinking countryside. I have been asked to give the countryman's view of the matter, which, of course, is literally right up my street. I want to do it, and I should be able to do it fairly easily, but the devil of it is that at each attempt I find it more and more difficult. In spite of all my efforts to the contrary I find myself writing such bad tempered stuff ; and I have enough sense to know that bad temper is worse than useless.

The trouble is that the countryman's attitude to the countryside is so widely different from the townsman's. To the former it is a business ; to the latter it is a playground. Indeed, the difference is even wider. Both parties want something from the countryside. The countryman is reasonable in that he wants something in return for something—to wit, the investment of his brains and his brawn and his capital. In contrast, the townsman wants something for nothing ; and, seeing that he outvotes the countryman by something like thirteen to one, usually he gets it.

In so doing I must admit that he gets my goat also, and how to keep this fact out of this chapter on the subject I do not know. I have a good mind not to try. They want the countryman's view. Why not let them have it undiluted ?

Of course, if I do that I shall most likely be in direct contradiction to some of the other writers of the book. But does that matter ? I do not think so ; for, to my mind, the freedom to express one's views which England grants to everyone is the hall mark of her greatness.

It was a conversation with a lad of twenty which has made me decide that this is so. He told me that he had had rampant socialism pumped into him at his school, and that after six months in Germany he had just returned home a confirmed fascist. This apparently was why he had been drawing me so cleverly concerning my views as to the future of England's countryside.

" In everything you say," he said, " you prove yourself to be a believer in fascism. You are pleading for a proper recognition of the countryside by the state."

" But I'm no fascist," I cut in. " God forbid. I cannot stand the thought of a dictatorship by either fascism or socialism. Neither will work in England. We're too sensible. We prefer the middle course."

Then I told him of my difficulties with regard to writing the chapter on the countryman's view, mentioning that I should be sure to disagree with some of the other writers.

" You see," I said, " I shall put forward that the farmer should have the right to order uninvited and non-paying visitors off his land, and someone, possibly my friend, C. E. M. Joad, may plead that the land should be used mainly for people in short pants to run about on."

" Ah !" he said. " Joad ! The first on a lamp-post when the balloon goes up."

And then I blew up, good and hearty.

" Thus proving, my lad, that you and your fascist friends recognize your intellectual inferiority to Joad. That you cannot face him in argument. That you fear his brain and therefore must needs destroy the container of it. The only thing you can do is to hang him ! What an admission of weakness ! What an admission that you are merely clumsy loutish bullies ! And the ultra communistic socialists are on a par with you. When their balloon goes up I suppose that I shall adorn a lamp-post ?"

" Now look here, no country can progress in that fashion

In fact, that fashion won't even get rid of the supposed
nuisance dictatorships wish to destroy. It will merely
perpetuate it and make it stronger. And England doesn't
do things that way. We've too much sense. We let our
extremists say what they like, and choose the middle course.
For instance, England will let Joad, or anyone who so wishes,
write reams about the land belonging to the people ; about
the divine right of our pavement-worn town population to
do just what they like in God's green England during their
scanty leisure ; about the necessity for everybody to enjoy
the wind on the heath no matter what any farmer may
think ; and so on. At the same time she will permit me
to blow off a lot of bad-tempered steam concerning the bad
manners of the town trespasser ; about the colossal
importance of farmers ; about the unfairness of the existing
law of trespass ; and to express the wish that I had the
right to kick hard up the behind all folk who trespass on my
farm. Which, my lad, I often yearn to do."

Here I paused for breath, which enabled him to say,
" And what then ? What does your wonderful England
do about it ?"

" Do ? My and your—don't forget that—wonderful
England just grins at both our splutterings, and somewhere
about half way between them she finds a workable solution.
And she doesn't find it by means of logic, my lad, but by
means of magic, the magic that is England, the wonderful
quality of tolerance ; which, while she hangs on to it and
keeps all extremists in their places by letting them spit out
their venom as and when they please, will enable her to
lead the world, not only materially but spiritually."

" And where do I find this magical quality ?" he asked.

" Anywhere in England. Machines have muted it a

trifle in the towns, but it still speaks in the countryside."
I told him. " Go and work on a farm. Learn to ride and
go hunting. Play cricket for a village team. Failing all
else, join the territorial army. In every case you will find
the only system of living which works decently, a proper
blend of autocracy and democracy which is flavoured with
a sense of humour. You've been to school and you've been
to Germany. But as an Englishmen you aren't half-
educated yet. Go and learn something about the English
countryside, which is still the real England."

It says much for his manners that he took my ranting in
good part, merely mourning that I was a good fascist
wasted. But I have since learned that he is learning to ride,
which is bound to teach him the virtue of the middle course.
Well, to quote the screen Henry the Eighth, " The things I
do for England !"

*   *   *   *   *   *

A friend of mine has just told me a great tale concerning
one of his horse-dealing escapades. Some years ago, while
buying cattle in Ireland, he was so taken with the look of
one young hunter that he bought it for twenty-five pounds,
shipped it home, and turned it out. At that date he was
a good deal younger than he is now, and fancied his riding
capabilities not a little ; so on his first free evening he
proceeded to try out his purchase. But I had best tell the
tale in his own words.

" He stood as quiet as a lamb while I bridled and saddled
him," he said, " an' so I took him out into the paddock
thinkin' everything were goin' to be all honey. He stood
quiet while I got up, an' then I found meself on the ground.
I picked meself up, spit the mud out o' me mouth, an' looked

at him. An' there he stood, a nice quiet hoss, waitin' fur me to get up again.''

" He looked so blame quiet that I got up again, and picks meself out o' the mud as before. An' there he stood as mild as milk. ' Blast you !' I says, 'I'll have another go.' Which I did wi' the same result. So I chucked it fur that day, and thought it over.''

" Well, I didn' like to be beat, so I went through the same didos wi' him most evenin's fur a month or more, an' I never stayed on him more'n thirty seconds at a stretch. So then I gi'ed it up. Makes your guts so sore to get chucked off three or four times every night. ' Sides I wur busy along then.''

" Some weeks afterwards a cunnin' lookin' li'l feller called, an' said, ' I hear, Mr. Blank, that you got an 'oss as you cain't ride.' Hell of a thing to say to a young man, wasn't it ?''

I nodded in sympathy. " What did you answer ?" I asked.

" Oh, I pleaded guilty. ' Yes ! ' I says. ' I got a hoss as I can't ride, an' neet can you.' He laughed at this, so I bet him a quid that he couldn' ride him either, an' the fool took it. We saddles M'Nabs nice an' quiet, an' I give Clever Dick a leg up. He went through the air like the young man on the flyin' trapeze, lands awkerd, an' breaks his wrist. I draws me quid all right, but 'twer discounted through havin' to drive 'tother to hospital.''

" Well, after that I made quite a bit o' cash bettin' folks as thought they could ride better'n me that they couldn' stick on him. Some were hurt, an' some werden, but all were beat. But I got tired o' havin' folk call, an' chip me about havin' a hoss I couldn' ride, so I decided to break the devil to plough. Mind you, there were no vice in him. He used to chuck 'em off, an' stand quiet for 'em to git up again. A real nice-mannered hoss."

"But before I could find time to break him to harness a civil spoken gentleman called one evenin' an' trotted out the same openin'. But I were too quick for him. He hadn' got no further than ' I hear Mr. Blank,' when I cut in wi' ' that I got a hoss as I can't ride, an' this time I've said it fust, see.' "

"He saw I were a mite hippy, so he apologized, an' asked if he could try. So, after raisin' the stakes to five pound, I agreed, and we went through the same giddy-go-round. But this gentleman wasn't hurt neet scared. He paid up the fiver, an' asked if he could have another go. 'Don't understand it,' he said. ' The horse is quiet enough. Look at his eye,' Well, he come off three more times, an' each time the hoss stood like a lamb for him to get up again. And then what's think ?"

"Goodness knows, Tom," I answered. " The whole business sounds like a fairy tale."

"Yes, I know, but 'tis gospel none the less. Well, he brushed hisself down, an' asked me how much I wanted for the hoss. You know that fair done me, for nobody hadn' ever bin fool enough to ask that question afore. Howsomever, I pulled meself together an' asked him forty quid. An' wi'out battin' an eyelid he bid me thirty. ' Your hoss, guvner,' I said quick, an' next day a hoss-box came for him."

"Well, you got out of a bad deal all right, as usual, Tom," I said. " Do you ever lose money dealing ?"

"Pretty near always," he grinned. " An' this time I were the mug."

"How ? You only paid twenty-five for him, and you

won all kinds of money in bets, besides getting shot of a wrong un at thirty quid,"

" Jist so. But the matter o' a twelvemonth atterwards I were up in Tattersalls. On'y looked in casual like as I had an hour to spare. An' what's think ? They were sellin' my hoss. I knowed him in a minnit."

" An' he were knocked down for three hindred an' twenty guineas," he added gloomily.

" How and why ? " I asked.

" Oh, I soon found that out. I spied the gentleman who'd bought him. Lookin' jist about pleased wi' life, he were. An' I went up an' asked him outright. ' Come on,' I said. ' I'm the mug, but how did you manage it ?' An' then he told me. Apparently breakin' an' makin' fust class hunters was his trade. The hoss behaved wi' 'em jist like he did wi' me. Chucked 'em off reg'lar. An' each time they put up more lead on him. Presently come the day when he were carryin' so much lead that he jist couldn' chuck off his jockey, an' once that happened he gi'ed up trying' an' were as good as gold. Ye see, I knowed all along that he were a nice quiet hoss. But to think I sold him for thirty quid !"

I must have looked my disbelief, for he said, " Ah ! You do think I'm just tellin' the tale, don't you ?"

" No-o-o," I answered. " I believe you, but I'm wondering if many other folk would, for it's altogether too glorious a story. Can I pass it on, Tom ?"

" Provided you keep my name out of it," he said. " I don't want folks to know what a mug I am."

And as his name is not Tom and he does not live anywhere near me I think I have obeyed his instructions to the letter.

I see that many of my neighbours have already turned their cows out to grass ; but, in spite of the feeling of inferiority which this engenders, I shall keep my dairy herd in hay and cake for another week. My water-meadows carry a good bite of grass, but only a few weeks ago they were under water. To-day they are very wet and soft, and still the rain comes down. Was ever a dairy farmer so tantalized ? To have some early grass and to be unable to feed it !

I can remember turning cows out to grass in February on one or two occasions, and this annual event being postponed until almost the end of April ; but usually it is lack of keep which delays spring grazing. Well, this year, a spring which looked like being a late one, has suddenly become early, and there is a green countryside no matter where I look. I should imagine that few folk can remember a better prospect for a wealth of grass and hay. But once again it will be the weather in May which will tell the tale. For myself, I could wish for some fine weather now and for some warm wet in May, a thing which rarely happens in my district. But wishing is no good ; we shall have to take what comes and do the best we can with it.

Easter Allsorts

At last it is dry overhead, and getting drier under foot ; and along with this pleasing change in the weather has come that east wind we should have had in March. Consequently it is rather cold, but who cares ? At long last we can get on with the work, and if we do that we shall not feel the cold.

To-day the outdoor herd came down into the valley, a thing which pleased both the cows and their attendants. For one thing the outfit is now much nearer the men's cottages, and for another grass feed means that hay hauling will soon be reduced to almost nothing.

The remainder of the oats have been put in, but the grass seeds are still to sow. Usually I put in my grass seeds at the time of sowing spring corn, but this year the job is too rough ; so I am leaving their sowing until the oats are up. This late sowing of grass seeds is a trifle risky, but another harrowing and rolling will help the oats. After all, farming of any type is just one fool risk after another.

*   *   *   *   *   *

Just now we are living in a state of suppressed excitement, for Glory's foal, which I have presented to Pam, is due to arrive. At least, mathematically it should have been here three or four days ago, but in my own judgment it is still a full week away. However, its owner is in such a state of mind over her property's non-arrival, that she worries the whole household and visits the prospective mother at every possible opportunity. It is useless for the

old dairyman to tell her to " let she bide, missie "; for the
groom-gardener to prophesy yet another foal-less fortnight ;
or for me to attempt to slip into the house when I return
home late at night without first visiting the stables.

Even yesterday night, when I arrived home from town
rather Irishly at two o'clock this morning, as soon as my
steps left the garage a small voice came from upstairs
window, saying, " Daddy ! You must have a look at Glory
to see she's all right." Never was a foal so eagerly expected,
and never in my experience has one seemed so loath to visit
this work-a-day world. Still, sooner or later he or she will
have to make his or her bow, to quote the drowner, " As
sure as God made little apples." It occurs to me that I
have never yet discovered any explanation why the making
of *little* apples by the Almighty is considered so certain.
For myself, I have an equal faith that He will make big
ones as well.

*　　*　　*　　*　　*　　*

Easter, the first general holiday of the year, is always
looked upon by townsfolk as a country one. The seaside
still wears its winter frown ; cricket, tennis, and other
summer pleasures have not yet arrived ; indoor amusements
are beginning to pall ; but after a long winter in town most
people feel that a breath of fresh air is essential. So the
majority of townsfolk decide to leave the man-made town
at Eastertime, and to visit the country in order to admire
the work of a vastly superior craftsman.

Undoubtedly such a decision is a wise one. In spite of
modern building and other forms of progress which have
defaced so many of England's one-time mellow fields, there
is still some countryside remaining ; and never is it more
lovely than at this season. Once more the Easter holiday

will enable many people to meet again and others perhaps
to meet for the first time a very lovely thing—green
England in the spring of the year. A few weeks ago, after
one of the longest and most uncomfortable winters on
record, spring came to the countryside in a great hurry.
Suddenly there was green everywhere—that green which
brings tears to the eyes of every returning exile when
his ship brings him first in sight of his homeland, that green
which no painter has ever reproduced on canvas successfully.

But although in some measure spring has fulfilled her
age-old Easter promise, this year she has done so with less
than her customary grace. At first coming she wept
incessantly ; and now, in April, when she has begun to
preen a little, there is much to criticize in her behaviour.
True, she is now making up her face with that guinea-a-
bushel powder which she should have used in March, but for
some reason or other she must needs use the cold powder
puff of an east wind with unseasonable and unmaidenly
vigour.

As a result, unless the wind changes, this Easter outdoors
must be an overcoat and muffler holiday, and the gnats and
warmth and shirtsleeves of last year can be only a regretful
memory. Another change will be that the town visitor
to rural England will find most of his country cousins hard
at work. Whilst he admires spring's natural loveliness and
so regains for a short time that feeling of wistful wonder
which to most adults is only a memory of childhood ;
while birds sing and mate on every bush and tree ; while
lambs run races together for the sheer joy of living ; while
a bracing wind sweeps over a green countryside ; those
who live by the land will be at work upon it. This
spring the local point-to-point must be given a miss ; this

Easter the village football teams will be minus some of their star players; and this week-end many regular patrons will be too tired in the evenings to journey by bus to the cinema.

Instead, the gardens and allotments will be clicking with busy workers like a hive of bees in May; and all day long horses and tractors and men will be moving slowly but surely "atheert an' across" the brown and barren fields. The land takes no heed of Bank Holidays, and those who serve it are very conscious just now that their spring work is all behind.

But, no matter how remote the field in which they toil, each time they turn their team or machine at the headland they will see strangers to the scene—people from towns, who have come by every known form of modern transport to admire the countryside at Eastertide. Possibly a few of these invaders will damage the thing they come to admire, but in the main their coming does much to bring about a closer understanding between town and country. Twenty years ago both old Bill Goodridge and the field he tilled were foreign to the inhabitants of England's towns. Now mechanical transport has introduced them to each other, and with the help of mutual courtesy they are fast becoming comparatively close neighbours and much better friends.

What matter if one is at work and the other on holiday? The former knows that in many ways he has the better life, and the latter derives considerable interest and pleasure from his holiday inspection of a great business in full swing. Alone amongst our industries farming permits all and sundry to watch its operations free of charge; and no park, no no matter how well it may be arranged for the visitor's delight, is half so attractive as a working countryside in

The Land takes no heed of Bank holidays

which man, bird, and beast are busy with their lawful avocations. Besides, those who have been forced by modern civilization to work with machinery, and bricks, and print derive great good from watching others working with natural live things.

There is, however, something else in the countryside, which town visitors will not find so pleasing. That field of last Easter is now a row of houses ; that lovely sweep of down now boasts an aerodrome, a roadhouse, or a pox of bungalows ; that charming winding lane has been straightened and widened ; and the countryside generally has been altered out of all recognition. A visit to the countryside this week-end should convince everybody that some control of these activities is very necessary, if their children's children are to enjoy their Easter holidays.

For Easter is, has been, and ever should be a country holiday for English people.

*   *   *   *   *   *

These diary books are snares and delusions to the writer, in that one's actions of to-day may give the lie to one's written promise of but a day or two before. For instance, the previous note suggested that while townsfolk would make holiday this Easter, the countryman would be forced to continue hard at work. Indeed, I was rash enough to write that he would be compelled to give his local point-to-point a miss in work's favour. And I still stick to it that most countrymen should have done this, and that many of them did do it ; but here I must confess that I provided the exception to prove the correctness of my ruling. In extenuation of my truancy to-day, Easter Saturday, I here plead that I laboured all day on Good Friday, and that this evening I am pounding a typewriter at ten p.m.

Anyway, rightly or wrongly, this afternoon my family and I attended the Wylye Valley Point-to-point. Brrh! And it was cold! A biting east wind swept across the course, and made the inside of one's car seem very inviting; so much so, that as we had a good place near the winning post, the ladies of the party remained in comfort, leaving Pam and me to brave the elements and place their bets as well as our own. Having financed my companion to the tune of one shilling per race, we set off full of enthusiasm.

In spite of the cold we had a grand time. We studied the horses with, I hope, a knowledgeable eye. We inspected several of the fences and estimated the probable capabilities of Master Thomas Webster to surmount them. We met and talked with numerous friends; and having placed our bets, returned to the car just before the start of most of the races.

One old friend asked Pam how long it would be before she was riding in the Ladies' Race, whereupon I explained that while the jockey was willing, the owner—to wit, her mother—had vetoed any thought of such a risky perform-ance.

" H'm!" he said. " Most mothers are like that. But you'd be a sight safer when ridin' this course on a good hoss than you'll be drivin' home with Daddy this evening."

Here may I say that he had the grace to qualify this by adding that he was casting no reflections on my capacities as a chauffeur, but rather on the dangerous state of the roads to-day. And the more I think about it, the more convinced I become that the road awheel is more dangerous than the fields on horseback. Still, I am entirely on her mother's side with regard to Pam's riding in point-to-points in years to come. During their season each year it is possible for man or woman by so doing to gain some little bubble glory ; but I am coward enough to admit that I do not think such reward worthy of the risk which gaining it entails.

To the best of riders may come that nasty fall, and those dashing married men who ride in point-to-points and steeplechases so gaily, do they ever give a thought to what their wives must suffer ? I write that because in the next car to ours was a young couple. After the fourth race they disappeared with a handbag, and just before the start of the fifth the lady returned alone to the car. Whereupon we put two and two together, and asked her if her husband was riding. She said that he was, and pointed to him lining up with the others for the start, explaining that it was his first race, and that he would probably not get round. It was too late to cross the course and back his mount for neighbourliness' sake, but our prayers went with him, in spite of the shillings we had invested on another horse.

What that little woman suffered during the race, good-ness only knows, but I saw her face. However, as the field was coming in to the last jump but one I was able to shout to her that her husband had the race in his pocket, barring accidents. What a fool I was to add the last two words ! But fate, a good horse, and some good horseman-ship sent him over the remaining fences, and up the straight several lengths in front of his nearest rival. He waved his whip in triumph as he passed his wife, and once again I stole a look at her face. If ever there was a happy, thankful woman at a point-to-point, she was in the next car ; and neither Pam, nor any of our party grudged the shillings we had lost on the horse which came in second.

But, quite frankly, I am not brave enough to sit in a

car and watch my only child ride that course or any other, and please God she will never want to do such a thing. And here, metaphorically perhaps but none the less in admiration, I take off my hat to that little woman and all others who are so much braver than I.

*   *   *   *   *   *

There seems to be no end to this rural junketing at Eastertide. Indeed, to-day, Sunday, I looked through my diary to find that every day this week I am booked for something, and that with the farm work all behind and my writing definitely in like case I shall have a dickens of a job to sandwich it all in. To-morrow I have promised Pam to hack with her some twelve miles, and, by kind permission of the owner of an estate, to leave her pony to spend the night in his stables, preparatory to a Pony Club Rally next day. Tuesday is to be dedicated to watching her performances there. Wednesday is our very own Wilton Hunt's Point-to-point, and we are due to attend the Salisbury Operatic Society's production of Rose Marie the same evening. Thursday my wife and I are booked to lunch with a neighbour. Friday is our Hunt Ball, and Saturday is the last meet of the season, quite close home.

Phew! There is not going to be much work done this week, that is very evident. And who said that living in the country was dull? Somebody who had never lived in rural England, and experienced its giddy whirl. Next Sunday I shall refuse to get up at all.

*   *   *   *   *   *

On Monday, Bank Holiday, the season started according to schedule. Pam and I hacked over to Thomas Webster's bed and breakfast accommodation, and thoroughly enjoyed the ride. A twelve mile hack across English country,

with a little girl for companion, and the sun shining
all the time, takes a lot of beating. One sees so much more
of rural England's activities in this fashion than one does
while doing the same journey in a car. That lonely-looking,
little-used green track is full of rural traffic. Round one
bend comes a flock of sheep ; round another a farm wagon
fills the lane, and perhaps one has to go back a hundred
yards or so to find a place wide enough to permit its passing.
Sometimes an enormous sow momentarily scares both horse
and rider. On occasion some patiently plodding cows
squelch by. One gives good-day to shepherd, keeper,
farmer, labourer, or poacher every half-mile. One obtains
the glimpse of a deer, and the brown flash of a fox ; pigeons
clatter from the trees overhead ; the occasional cock
pheasant explodes with his customary suddenness ; and
one's path is garnished with rabbits rabbits rabbits, rabbits
all the way.

In this fashion we arrived at our destination, to be
greeted with broad grins by the High Bird, who had driven
over in the car. Translated, this means our one and only
long-suffering groom-gardener. His name is Hibberd, but
Pam has long since honoured him with the more majestic
title. Having put the celebrated Thomas Webster to bed,
as Pam remarked, " still gutting", she and I set out for
home in the car, what time the High Bird clattered out of
the stable yard on Peter.

We chattered so much about the morrow's doings that
not until we were half way home did we discover that there
was a tea for all of us put up in the car ; so we cut corners
across country in order to share it with the High Bird and
Peter. I don't take sugar but Peter does. Altogether a
most satisfactory Bank Holiday, for the greatest number of

people we saw gathered together in one place was only four.

* * * * * *

As a farmer I sold my produce wholesale, as a milkman I sold it retail, but now as a writer I find that I not only sell the produce of my pen but that I am repeatedly forced to sell myself. Which, of course, sounds like the worst form of prostitution. Perhaps that is too harsh a description of the machinations of publishers and booksellers ; but I do sometimes feel that these friends of mine cause me to be exhibited to the public in the same fashion as livestock is exhibited at an agricultural show. Presumable I adorn the crossbred section of their show, being exhibited as a Wiltshire freak, by Poverty out of Farm—not, I think, the worst of pedigrees.

Personally I could bear these necessary trials of my calling with more equanimity if the majority of visitors to the show did not ask me, " And do you really farm ?"—the more especially as when I tell them that I " really do " they invariably look their disbelief.

I wish some of those Doubting Thomases could have seen me this morning. At six-thirty Charlie woke me with the news that he had a cow in a ditch, and that he reckoned, " 'twer a bad job." I scrambled on some clothes, gathered up the drowner, the High Bird, and a selection of ropes, and drove furiously up the lane.

Owing to the wet spring the pasture which the herd were using as a night ground had not dried out down the lower end, and there we found Daisy, up to her belly in mud and water, and looking half dead. There was no time to be lost, for Daisy was in no shape to give us any answer. We hitched a wagon line round her horns, and put another one behind her buttocks. And thereafter we pulled.

At first we failed to shift her, but the arrival of two more hands gave us just the extra power required. There was one awful moment when Daisy's neck was so stretched that it looked as though her head would part from her body, then there was a hollow squelch, some effort on her part, and out she came ; as the drowner put it, " Jist like pullin' a knife out o' butter."

If by butter he meant black mud, Charlie and I were covered in butter, and when we returned home our wives were not exactly pleased at the thought of such filthy garments going into the wash tub forthwith—Easter Monday having postponed this week's washing day until Tuesday. However, such jobs prove to me that I do "really farm," and this one gave me a grand appetite for breakfast. Incidentally, it will also touch my farming pocket, for I do not think that Daisy will pull through.

Thinking that twenty pounds had most probably gone west on the farm, I spent the remainder of the forenoon trying to discount the loss with my pen ; and after lunch set off with Pam and the High Bird to renew our acquaintance with Tom Webster. He was undeniably glad to see us, and behaved very well during the afternoon.

Why is it that children will always take instructions so much better from a stranger than from their own parents ? The Pony Club instructor was no respecter of persons. When any pony or its rider did not obey orders he voiced his displeasure. In fact, although he did not exactly shout it in their ears, he did say it very loud and clear. And was he obeyed ? With a click, in the same way that recruits obey a sergeant-major. In two hours he taught those children more about horsemanship than anyone else had taught them in the previous two years. Many other fond parents were present, and how we exulted at his methods!

"That's the stuff," said one father to me. "I wouldn't have missed this for anything. My kid's never been properly told off before. Do him a power of good."

I agreed with him, but when I asked him what sort of a show we parents would put up under the same teacher, he said, "God forbid! If I thought that was going to happen, I should make a bolt for my car at once. I wouldn't do it for a fiver."

But how the children enjoyed it. After an hour's riding-school work their teacher suggested that it was time to have a little fun, and led the way to some hurdles. "Let me see how you can jump," he said.

One after another the children jumped a hurdle, even Tom Webster sailing over to the manner born.

"Humph! Not so bad, but any fool can do that sort of thing," was the comment. "At a canter the pony jumps on his own. You don't make him. Let me see if you can jump that hurdle at a walk."

How he did it, I cannot make out, but in half an hour each one of those riders could walk his or her mount to within three yards of a three foot hurdle, and then squeeze him over like a cork. But at first every pony refused to perform such tricks, each according to their several ideas of such foolery. It would ill become me to describe other children's ponies' methods, so I will confine myself to those of Thomas Webster.

He walked towards the hurdle. Three yards away he stopped and grinned at it with a truly rocking-horse grin. Obeying orders, his mistress forced him towards the hurdle. In order to please the child he shuffled towards it, and stood there with the same fool grin on his fat white face. If his mistress wanted him to look over a hurdle, he was too great a gentleman to refuse. But his mistress, urged on by her instructor and the titters of the onlookers, wanted him to jump the said hurdle. This was absurd. No self-respecting pony could do such a thing without a decent run. However, repeated drummings of her heels on his ribs inferred that something further was expected of him. So he gravely placed one forefoot upon the hurdle, knocked it down, and then strolled calmly through the opening ; as if to say, " Mere child's play to a pony of my intelligence."

The hurdle was re-erected, and Master Tom was brought round to face it once more. But this time a strange voice was added to his rider's pleadings, a voice which held in it a note of command and the threat of worse to follow. Quite definitely this voice held a message for Master Tom, for he bundled over that hurdle in fine style, and thereafter continued so to do.

Everbody voted the whole afternoon great fun, and the riders all went home vowing to continue their ponies' education on strict Pony Club lines. Indeed, to-day has quite convinced me that in return for a subscription to the Pony Club parents, children, and ponies get wonderful value for money.

*　　*　　*　　*　　*　　*

An east wind still rules the whole world, so much so that while Pam and I went to the Wilton Point-to-point at Toyd to-day, the remainder of my household stayed at home and stoked the fire. Having both made money at the Wylye Valley, Pam and I naturally expected to do much better at our own hunt's meeting. We knew the horses, we knew the riders, we were on speaking terms with the huntsman, whips, and many owners and grooms. These advantages would overcome the cold, and great should be the spoil thereof. Alas ! Perhaps we knew too much, for when we left before the last race, we left several shillings behind us.

Still, we had great fun, and only left early because, as Peter is still lame, a friend had lent me an old steeplechaser to try, which the High Bird was going to hack home. Speculator was his name ; and, although his owner had prepared him for a race, he had decided not to run him. In consequence, he was so uppish in his behaviour when he set out that both Pam and I both speculated as to whether Speculator and the High Bird might not part company before long. So we left early, and by judicious cutting of corners in the car managed to watch their progress, which took place without any untoward happening.

By so doing we missed the best of the day, for in the last race a little black pony came in second. A bad second in terms of distance, perhaps, but such a good one for its size, I was told, to be greeted by cheers from everbody. So good was its performance that the farmer whose horse won the race gave up the cup to the owner of the pony. Now to do that sort of thing seems hardly logical. Here was a man who owned a horse, who had prepared it for this particular race, and managed to win it fairly and squarely. And he gives up the prize to the second ! It may not be logical, but then neither English farmers nor English hunting folk are logical. But they are English. Hence the action of the winner of the last race.

Just one more note—in spite of everything we could do, Daisy has passed out, and has been sent to the kennels.

*   *   *   *   *   *

The countryside is fairly going it this week. This morning in company with Pam I rode Speculator. He is an enormous horse, fully seventeen hands ; old, I grant, and more than a bit of a crock ; but can't he go ? He gives one the feeling of sitting on a train, and that there is nothing which he could not jump. But he dealt with my fifteen stone with such scant ceremony that I was filled with speculations—not so much as to his capabilities but as to mine. It is a wise man who knows his limitations.

And now the order has come down from upstairs that I must go and dress. Gosh ! I hope there will be a chance of some quiet bridge at this Hunt Ball, for I am too old for the customary caperings. In dancing I am that same wise man as I am with regard to my riding—I know my limitations.

*	*	*	*	*	*

Hunt Balls are enjoyable functions, chiefly, I think, because everybody is so friendly—one touch of horseflesh making everybody kin. So infectious was the gaiety yesterday evening that somehow or other I found myself dancing, or at least endeavouring so to do—I, who have not danced for years !

The original idea was that my wife and I would put in an appearance, stay long enough to greet our friends, and then silently steal away to bed, at least by half-time. But no ! Such were the friendliness and the fun that we were both dancing when the time was called, and both regretted that the " King " came so early in the morning.

And none of the company present finished up the evening, or rather morning, so fittingly as my wife and I. When we were returning home about 4 a.m. we saw the lantern of the High Bird flickering across the lane outside the buildings. He greeted us with the news that the anxiously awaited thoroughbred foal had just arrived safely. Whereupon my wife, regardless of her evening finery, made a sloshy bran mash, and came over to see it administered and to admire the latest addition to the family. I have never before tried to teach a newly-born foal to suck, while I have been arrayed in tails and a white waistcoat, and to be honest I don't recommend the garb, but we managed the business all right, and went to bed feeling very satisfied with life. Incidentally, for two pins I would christen that foal, Dancer.

* * * * * *

I scribbled the previous note after breakfast on Saturday morning ; and now, this evening, when I am practically laid out after hunting, the labourer returns to his task. What with introducing Pam to her new foal, coping with Speculator all day, and bearing up after last night's revelling, I am feeling decidedly piano.

Hunt Balls are enjoyable functions, but they make middle-age realize its years. One is so gay while the band is playing and the champagne is flowing, but one feels so old next morning. And when next morning means, as it did to-day and always should, that delightful holiday meet to finish the season, one feels older still. Anyway, I did and do.

The trouble was that Speculator didn't feel a bit old, and I was in no shape to deal with his exuberance. Silly old fool! His behaviour and mine were in such direct contrast that one of my ribald companions of last night remarked that he hoped I looked more at home in front of a microphone than I did in the saddle. What it is to have friends in the countryside, and what a horrible place the countryside would be without them !

But who resents such truthful and friendly criticism ?

I don't. When one sees over a hundred riders, of all shapes, sizes, ages, and capabilities, turning out to wind up the season in style and to show that a little thing like dancing until the small hours cannot damp their enthusiasm, one feels more convinced than ever that the English countryside is still very much alive. Besides, although I may be a very bad rider of old horses, no one can say that I haven't got a young horse in stable. Incidentally, although that same young horse is all legs, as far as I and one or two knowledgeable friends can judge, he is put together on the right lines.

Although we did not kill or experience anything special in the way of runs, to-day's hunting provided something new for me, and, I should imagine, for most folk present. By invitation the Wylye Valley hunt joined us at the meet, and the two packs were handled as one. Two to one is not supposed to be fair, but our Grovely foxes dodged the double-sized pack quite easily. It occurs to me that the number of times I have seen or heard of a Grovely fox being bustled out of the wood and killed can be counted on my two hands.

But the most interesting thing to me was to see the mixed pack parted at the end of the day. On an open down the majority of each pack knew the respective voices of their particular Master and huntsman so well that they separated themselves, leaving only three or four goats in each flock of well-trained sheep. And most of these renegades gave very little trouble when their friends made contact with them, only one or two needing to be forcibly dragged from their new companions. Incidentally, a man in breeches and top boots carrying a foxhound over fifty yards of down has his hands quite full.

Speculator has quietened down considerably for two reasons. One is that we are not corning him up to further zest ; and the other that two nights ago at dinner his owner gave me the key to the trouble. To be quite fair he tried to do this at Toyd, but I was too thick to take it in.

Part of the charm of horses is that by comparison with a motor car no two are alike. Indeed, a friend of mine who employs a groom-chauffeur once told me that for this reason he could never get a man who could fill both roles adequately. Apparently, the perfect groom gave him repeated shocks while acting as a chauffeur, and the perfect chauffeur never realized the superiority of the horse over the car.

" The man I've got now isn't bad," he explained. "He's very good with cars and a good driver. He also does the horses not too badly. But I cannot knock it into his head that if the car is damaged I can buy another identical vehicle. But that if a horse becomes unfit for work I cannot buy another one just like it for all the gold of the Indies."

Speculator's particular idiosyncrasy is that his elbow rubs the girth when either walking or trotting. Consequently, when ridden with a girth of ordinary width, he refuses either to walk or to trot. True, thus equipped, he will stand still, which is a comfort, and he will gallop like a train ; but to walk sedately and permit me to admire the countryside, as is my habit far more than galloping at speed, he will not.

But, placed in accordance with his owner's instructions, two pieces of bicycle inner tube worked wonders. They managed to constrict a web girth to a bare two inches of smooth rubber where his elbow rubbed, and transformed a worry into a pleasure. Even so, I am convinced that

Speculator is too much of a man for me. He is bitten with the modern craze for speed, whereas I am fast becoming an anachronism in connection with this feature of modern life. Besides I have not enough work to keep him subdued, to my needs; the High Bird has far too much gardening in front of him to warrant wasting his valuable time in exercising my horse when my work prevents me from riding; and Speculator is far too big and mighty for Pam's little wrists.

So I have decided not to buy him, and he returns to his owner to-morrow with many thanks for the loan. He is a good old horse, but I am a bad old horseman, so it is best that we part friends in my way instead of parting company suddenly as enemies in his.

*   *   *   *   *   *

The weather is a trifle warmer, so Glory and her foal are able to spend the day in the paddock near the house. What funny things young foals are! At birth they look to be all joints, and to be fitted with such awkward stilts that the uninitiated might well doubt whether such an animal could walk. And yet at forty-eight hours old they can gallop at speed!

I was showing Glory's foal to a school teacher friend the other day, and during its gallivanting round the paddock I pointed out that its mother always managed to get between her baby and the fence, in order to protect it from its own speed. This is necessary, as very young foals are not fitted with effective brakes.

" I wish human mothers took as much care of their offspring," she murmured gloomily. " A village school teacher is practically a foster mother nowadays—certainly a nanny. What with milk and cod liver oil teachers will soon have to agree to take babies from the month."

All Flesh is Grass

And presumably the day comes to all flesh when it is cut down to wither and die. This gloomy thought has been ever present in my mind during the last few days, for I have been wondering whether my time was not very near. Whether it was the early morning stable work with Glory's foal, the dancing beforehand, the hunting afterwards, or one of my many other rural junketings which was responsible I know not, but for several days I have been in bed with the " flu."

Apparently influenza is no respecter of persons, dates, or weather ; and so, during the first decent week of this year I have been laid by the heels. Work, pleasure, appetite, thought even, all had to come to a full stop during those glorious final days of April. Outside the sun shone and the birds sang; indoors a limp imitation of a man clung to a hot water bottle in a darkened room, wondering just how any bird could sing. Influenza is like that. For the first few days its awfulness is so vast that everything else in the world is dwarfed into insignificance. But when the worst is over, even though weakness still confines him to the house, the farmer begins to farm again—farming being worse than influenza, in that one never gets to the end of it.

And now, even though I have recovered sufficiently to be able to think without my head going round, I am still upstairs, and obliged to content myself with the view from my bedroom window and the reports of my various henchmen. These, strange to say, seem really concerned about my health. Queer, how that sort of thing pleases one, but there is no doubt that it does do so.

But even from my eyrie I can see that the countryside has made great progress in a week. The whole world has been getting green at top speed all right, but I take my hat off—at least I would if I wore one upstairs—to one particular beech tree in a mile long row of others. Alone amongst its companions it has burst into leaf, and I can see and admire its brave challenge to spring—one lone, pale-green banner, flaunting gaily in a long rank of dour mail-clad knights. Why this particular beech should have come out a full week in advance of its fellows I cannot think, but the sight of it has cheered me up considerably, and the first time I go outdoors I shall journey up the hill to say thank-you to it. The early green of the beech is, I think, one of the loveliest shades of spring, and soon it will be seen all over England.

*   *   *   *   *   *

Another cheering thing has been to watch the antics of the foal, as it plays around its dam in the paddock outside my window. Really, when foals are first born they look so awkward as to warrant the description, ludicrous. They are all legs and joints. But after a week it is amazing how they can manage themselves on such clumsy-looking stilts.

It is many years now since a foal was bred on this farm, and a conversation I overheard this afternoon reminded me of this fact and also of how mechanized farming has become. Some children were discussing the foal.

"I tell 'ee 'tis a baby 'orse, laid down. That be 'is mother."

"Garn ! They don't 'ave baby 'osses nowadays."

"Don't 'em ! Thellak ! 'Ee've got up. Now, 'oo wur right ? That be a baby 'orse."

Garn they don't 'ave baby 'osses now a days.

Then there was a long pause, while the foal sucked his mother.   And then I heard, " Billy, be you sure that be a baby 'orse ? "

And they were rural children !   It strikes me that unless we are very careful there will soon be a generation of children in both country and town to whom the story of the animals in the ark will be meaningless.

Even so, I doubt whether many folk will worry very much ;   for the Budget debate this week has shown me that there are a good many people in this country who think only in terms of town.   While baiting the Chancellor of the Exchequer about raiding the Road Fund several politicians of all parties suggested that all the main roads in the country should be flood-lit at night from end to end ;   and that it was criminal to rob the Road Fund until this necessary improvement had been effected.

Words fail me.   Is it their aim to make of all England one continuous built-up area ?   Do they want to see the whole of this island under the sway of illuminated mechanical carnival from dusk till dawn ?   Is their ideal an England which is one glorified and magnified Piccadilly Circus ?   Have they no appreciation of natural quiet and natural velvet dark ?   Must every day be noisy and every night a gaudy one ?   Are they insane, or merely drunk with machinery ?

Whew !   And I said words failed me !   Evidently they don't, but my excuses must be the after effects of influenza, and that I should hate to see all England a town of pavements, lights, and man's cleverness, an England in which everything happens according to the ordering of mankind. Such, I imagine, is the opinion of all countryfolk, and perhaps it would be well for the few of us who remain to recognize the motive which urges these town politicians to plead for such things to come to pass.

It is that the majority of town dwellers fear and mistrust and therefore hate the countryside and would like to see an England in which light and dark, hill and dale, ruts and puddles, rain and drought, and countless other natural inequalities were swept away in favour of State regimentation and artificial levelling in every phase of life. For the natural inequalities of the little bit of countryside which remains and the mode of life which they demand breed the individualist, the John Bull ; a figure which has become very out of date in English life to-day. They do not bother to draw him in cartoons now ; instead we have Strube's Little Man, the product of the town. He it is who must have his England lit up from end to end ; because, forsooth he is afraid of everything natural, even of the dark.

* * * * * *

I'm not so sure that I don't enjoy being ill—I don't, of course, mean the really ill part of it, but the convalescent period which follows. All too rare in this life comes the day when one can do nothing and feel safe from the criticisms of one's friends and enemies and the pricks of one's own conscience. And usually when such a happy state of things occurs the weather is hopeless.

But last week was ideal. Weather perfect, surroundings ditto, and myself sloth personified. I just meandered round the farm watching other folk at work, and I defy anyone to suggest a more pleasing way of spending a day. Sometimes I wandered on the top of the downs ; from where I noticed that the brown patches in the countryside were getting fewer, and that green was covering everything. Above my head I noticed that lovely English clear blue sky of weather set fair. I'm a poor hand at colours, but I should call it turquoise blue, and the funny thing about it is that every blooming colour in the world goes well with it. A red cricket ball, the silver steel aeroplane, yellow thatch, red tiles, grey stone, green grass, there is no colour that does not go with turquoise blue of a May sky.

Down in the meadows I noticed all sorts of things, a moorhen's nest, a cuckoo in flight, a water rat swimming, and a trout rising. This last sent me home to overhaul my tackle, for although I am a bad fisherman, I am one of that select body of craftsmen, not the wet fly, nor the dry fly, but the very fly fisherman.

By that I mean that I use fishing as an excuse to spend a long lazy day in the meadows. To me a day's fishing is composed as follows—a complete absence of hurry, much quiet meandering, more careful sitting-down, a snooze or two, many pipes, much beer, a good lunch, some esoteric conversation with keeper, drowner, or dairyman, with here and there a little gentle fishing to flavour the whole dish. With or without fish in his basket the man who follows this recipe will leave the river at dusk a happy man. Why? Because he has had sense enough to be content with what the river and meadows had to give him, and did not try to extract too much more by personal effort. Because he is a very fly fisherman, the only type who should be allowed to enjoy the delights of the English chalk stream.

*   *   *   *   *   *

Now that the thick end of the spring sowing has been accomplished one wonders each day just for how long the wind will remain in the north-east. Dry weather was wanted, goodness knows, but the cold wind which has accompanied it has brought all growth to a standstill. Once again the dry has paid and overpaid the wet.   In fact when a neighbour asked me, apropos of his personal desire for a good rain, just what branch of farming a good rain would harm, I could not think of one.   For with rain a rise in temperature must come, and everything on the farm needs that badly.

When we get these barren periods in the spring of the year I go about my farm wondering, ay doubting, whether the age old promise of harvest can be fulfilled as it has been ever since the world began.   Can that barren pasture at the end of April be a decent cut of hay by the first week in June ?   Can that faint green tinge over the land be a waving sea of golden wheat in a little better than three months' time ?   Can that brown arable field show the ash blonde of ripe oats at the same date in August ?   It all seems impossible, but yet faith tells me that it will happen according to Earth's ancient and unalterable schedule.   No one, I imagine, will accuse me of boasting, if I suggest that these marvellous things happen here in more charming fashion than anywhere else in the world.

*   *   *   *   *   *

Pam and I decided some days ago to christen Glory's foal, Farmer's Glory.   His mother's official title is Sea of Glory, and his father's is Fortune of War.   Farmer's Glory was a great piece of good fortune for me, so the name seems to suit admirably.   Accordingly we wrote to Messrs. Weatherby in order to register the name, only to be greatly disappointed.   Someone else has forestalled us, and our chosen name is not now available.

This seems a bit hard.   Dash it !   There may be no copyright in titles, but I do think that we should have first claim to this one, especially as this foal is the first thoroughbred which we have either bred or owned. Weatherby's have asked for a few alternative names, so we have sent up, Moonraker, Buttercup Joe—the foal is a chestnut—and Lucky Wave, in that order of precedence. I also put a line in my letter, asking who had pinched the name Farmer's Glory, and whether there was any chance of him or her relinquishing it in our favour.

But even if the foal is nameless for the moment, his education has begun. We put a wide webbing halter on him this evening, and tried to lead him. At first he objected most strongly, and twice he upset his little self in his efforts to get away. But after a few minutes struggling he came to hand like the thoroughbred he is, and great was his owner's joy. She has resolved that he must have five minutes education every evening after her own has finished for the day ; and, if she keeps to it, there is no doubt that future owners of her foal will benefit greatly. " Catch 'em young and treat 'em kindly " is the best method of educating any young animal.

*   *   *   *   *   *

It is a long time since I saw the New Forest looking quite so lovely. I drove through it the other day, and was charmed with every mile. The greens and purples and ambers of new foliage were blended and contrasted by the hand of the Master, while the gorse flamed in glory beneath them. If the old saying " When the gorse is out of bloom, kissing's out of fashion " has any truth in it, kissing must be in full swing in the Forest just now.

A rather utilitarian friend who was with me pointed out that, although the land looked valueless for farming, wherever a cottage had been built, a fertile garden could be found alongside it. From this he argued that all the forest could be reclaimed, and turned into productive farming land.

Well, I daresay it could be so transformed, but I very much doubt whether it would pay the nation to effect this transformation. Some sort of natural farming is carried on in the Forest—one sees Guernsey cows, pony mares and foals, and really gargantuan pigs all over the place—and alongside this type of farming thousands of townsfolk enjoy the glory of the forest, without seemingly doing much harm to its agriculture. But if the Forest were reclaimed, and every acre of it under high farming, what then ? A gain in money, perhaps but a big loss in other values ; for in consequence, thousands of townsfolk would lose a health-giving and altogether lovely pleasure ground. On balance I am convinced that the nation would be much worse off. Think of it ! The gorse would be gone ; and one kiss in the forest is worth two in the cinema.

So much for a pleasant drive in England's countryside during May. Now for a another journey, during which I discovered something which left a nasty taste in my mouth. Four of us lost our way trying to take a short cut with a car across country, and after driving for miles along a green track, we turned into a narrow metalled lane. A few hundred yards of this brought us to a farmhouse and range of buildings. We skirted these, and set off along another and more-used lane, which evidently led to a main road.

Then we saw a man running from a field towards us. We pulled up, and in a moment or two he put his head into the car. He asked us if we had come to distrain on his cows for tithes, informing us that by the appearance of the car he reckoned we had come to spy out the land on behalf of the Church.

" Well!" said my friend who was driving. "I've been taken for all sorts of things in my time, but this is the first time I've been taken for a bum bailiff."

It is perhaps hardly my province to go into the vexed question of tithe, but I would point out that for such a thing as I have described to happen in England in the twentieth century is a grave criticism of our modern civilization. If it were not so tragic, it could be truthfully described as ridiculous. Many years ago in the Wild and Woolly West of America the farmer looked upon the chance visitor as a raiding enemy, but for the same thing to happen in England to-day! Help!

So, for goodness' sake, let both parties to the tithe dispute try to effect a settlement, which shall put an end to the childish practices and bad feeling which have obtained for so many years. I say this, not because I have anything to gain from the tithe bill which is now before parliament—as a tenant farmer I shall not gain one penny from its passing—but because during the past few years the behaviour of both tithe-owners and tithe-payers have brought nothing but discredit to the English nation. Besides, I resent being taken for a " bum bailiff " during my drives through our lovely land at any season of the year, and especially when May is smiling everywhere.

* * * * * *

To-day a friend called and asked if I would come for a drive, pointing out that it was a gorgeous afternoon, and that he had something which he wished to show me. This man's company and conversation are commodities which no one should refuse when the chance comes to enjoy them, so, of course, I played truant from work. This friend, to my knowledge, never does anything without a definite purpose, so, as his car slid off, I inquired just what particular form of devilment he had in mind for the afternoon.

" Goin' to improve your education," he said. An' God knows it needs it. You stick indoors far too much. Damn it ! You can't turn stuff out all the time ; you must put some in occasionally, else the well'll soon run dry. I'm takin' you to have a look at the wild land down in Blankshire."

" Wild land in Blankshire ?" I queried.

" Yes ! Thousands of acres of it. Good farming land that's been let run wild for about twenty years. Bloody scandal !"

" But why ?" I asked. " Surely that sort of game doesn't pay ?"

" Pay ? No, 'course it don't. But when a man lets a quarrel obsess him, he don't give a damn about profit for himself as long as he can make his enemy drop money."

Apparently, rather than pay tithe some landowner had let his estate go derelict, and it was this land which I was to be shown. And we found it. Thousands of acres of it. Farm after farm after farm. All derelict. All left to rabbits, thorn bushes, and weeds. Farms which in my boyhood had employed dozens of men, kept pedigree prize-winning flocks, and produced wheat and barley and oats of first-class quality. And now, nothing but the abomination of desolation !

I spoke my disgust aloud, and asked what the farm labourers thought of such a tragedy. " Let's draw the next village, and ask," said my friend.

This we did, and talked for some time with an agricultural labourer of the good old-fashioned type. He mourned the present condition of the acres on which his father had been a head-shepherd of a good flock ; he regretted the absence of farm employment in consequence ; but when I suggested that he probably did not hold a very high opinion of the man who was responsible, his reply staggered me.

" Oh, I dunno," he said. " I ain't got nothin' to say agen Mr. So-and-so. He showed they passons one."

And that remark showed me that notwithstanding a lot of unfair hot air which is levied against the tithe-owner there is a real grievance in the countryside about this question of tithe. Otherwise, why should an agricultural labourer consider that a landowner in his battle with the Church over tithe had more than condoned his neglect of so many acres of England ?

For myself, I have always considered tithe, from the point of view of the man who buys land, to be a legal debt which the buyer must meet. That the Church has possibly evaded her one-time liabilities in the matter of education, hospital work, and care of the poor, and at the same time hung on to the tithe is surely a matter for her dignitaries' and members' consciences ; but none of these things can alter the fact that the buyer of land agreed to shoulder the burden of tithe when he bought it. That, owing to the extraordinary depression in British agriculture since the 1925 Tithe Settlement, a review of the whole question and a scaling down of the value of tithe to a point more in relationship with the present prices of farm produce would not only be fair to farming but also of benefit to everybody concerned, I am convinced. But these folk who talk of abolition, with a view to the whole value of tithe finding its way into the pockets of landowners, are to my mind doing grave disservice to farming, and trying to use religious difference of opinion in order to enable them to dodge a legal

The good old-fashioned type.

debt.   These views, I know, are very unpopular with many farmers, but most of my farming friends who pay tithe, are in agreement with them—black legs in the eyes of the malcontents, possibly, but men who have no wish to evade liabilities which they incurred with their eyes open.

But to repeat, that farm labourer's answer proves to me that it is high time the contending parties in the matter of tithe were forced to come to some legal agreement which will end the bad feeling and undignified disturbances which have been carried on during recent years in different parts of rural England.   For this reason I have a notion that the proposed new Tithe Bill which is now being discussed is not very far off the mark ;   and the comment of a farming neighbour who is a fairly large tithe payer confirms this view.

" That ain't too bad a job at all," he said to me the other day.   " Both parties are grumblin' over it.   The tithe-owner says he's being robbed, and the tithe-payer says that the proposed reduction isn't half enough.   When two unreasonable and disgruntled parties are both dissatisfied with an umpire's award, you can bet your boots that it is a just one."

So much for tithe, which was perhaps the initial cause of the desecration of that large stretch of England which I saw this afternoon.   But what about the question of permitting land to remain derelict ?   I do not care what quarrel a landowner has with the Church ; but I do care that apparently he has the power to permit such treatment of England's lovely land to continue.   Somehow or other that power to do harm to the nation's one and only permanent asset, the land, should be taken away.

*   *   *   *   *   *

I have never been able to find out whether rhubarb is a

fruit or a vegetable, but I have long decided that, save in the form of jam, it is not worth eating. Let times be as bad as they can be, I would sooner starve than insult my inside with stewed rhubarb ; and I have noticed that those who do eat the stuff merely use it as a vehicle to carry enormous quantities of cream and sugar. So I was very amused this week at the remark of a neighbour, when his wife asked him whether he would have some stewed rhubarb. He surveyed the dish, and screwed up his face doubtfully.

" Ye-e-s," he said, " I will, but to finish the season."

To my mind the rhubarb season never ought to start.

     *   *   *   *   *   *

Why is it that women in connection with England's countryside, seem to possess a much poorer appreciation than men of the law of *meum et tuum ?* It is, I suppose, on all fours with their love of a bargain, for no woman of my acquaintance, either townswoman or countrywoman, thinks anything of deliberate stealing while she is walking or driving through the countryside.

" Why shouldn't I pick a few rhododendrons ?" a lady friend asked me the other day. " I only wanted a few blooms to put in my vases, and the keeper came up and spoke to me as though I were ten years old. Most rude he was."

" But don't you see," I argued, " that by stealing his employer's blooms you were putting yourself into the badly brought-up ten year old class ?"

And then of course, I caught it hot ; not only from my friend but also from my wife who informed me that I had no manners. So I meekly said that people who went about the countryside stealing had even less manners than I. And then, of course, I caught it hotter still.

But I don't care. I reckon that I suffered in a good cause. Why the dickens should people, and especially people who ought to know better, consider it all right to steal from farmers and landowners ? They pay nothing to see the wondrous spectacle of country England, and yet they must steal a bit of it at every visit. When I go to the cinema—and, mark you, I have to pay to witness the show it presents—I don't come home with a snippet of the carpet or a piece of the curtain.

Most men recognize the force of this argument and so refrain from stealing, but women don't. They continue to steal two pennyworth of blooms or foliage at every opportunity ; which is doubly queer when one considers that while so doing they usually wreck a 7s. 11d. pair of silk stockings.

*   *   *   *   *   *

A day spent at Fonthill Bishop has reminded me of the title of this chapter—that all flesh is grass. The other morning I drove down to that village in order to attend a Demonstration and Conference on Grass Drying, which was held there by kind permission of J. G. Morrison, Esq., M.F.H. The place was like a point-to-point meeting—nine hundred cars at an average of just over two people per car, makes the attendance about 2000.

Large farmers, small farmers, small-holders, landowners, agricultural students, budding farmers, everybody connected with farming was represented in force. Why ? Just because the principle behind this grass-drying idea is a sound one—to conserve at its maximum value the product of the most important of all farm crops in this country, GRASS. At the moment the equipment necessary to do this is too expensive save for the larger farmer, but no doubt in due time the artificial drying of grass will be made an economic proposition for the smaller farms. To repeat— when the principle of an idea is sound, man's ingenuity always finds a way to put that idea into operation. It is when the principle is unsound, that no planning can achieve success.

But whatever happens in the future concerning the artificial drying of grass, that gathering at Fonthill proved beyond all question just how important grass is in British farming. A demonstration with or a discussion on any other crop could not have got one quarter as many farmers together, not even if they had been paid five guineas per head to attend.

Of course, there are all sorts of things to be found out yet before every farmer will be drying his grass by artificial means—the effect of continued cutting on the pasture, or rather the temporary ley ; whether stock can be fed entirely on dried grass during the winter, or whether there must be some hay or straw in the ration to provide bulk ; and, last but not least, the effect on the artificial feeding stuff market if an increasing number of farmers cease to buy feeding stuffs owing to producing their own winter concentrates in the form of dried grass.

But here are a few obvious advantages of grass drying which spring to mind. The spreading out of one's summer work of storing winter fodder from May until September instead of that awful three weeks' rush of haymaking ; of being able to say, " That to you " to the British climate— a very satisfying thought this ; and the knowledge that one has said good-bye for ever to untidy pastures. These advantages, I think, outweigh any disadvantages, and there is no doubt that British farmers of all classes are keenly interested in this grass-drying idea, and are eagerly awaiting the time when it becomes a business proposition for the average size farm.

This afternoon's discussion was the first occasion on which I have had the pleasure of listening to Professor Stapledon. What a first-class political candidate he would make for any constituency; and especially for one in which the greater majority of the voters disagreed with the party's programme which he supported ! For he can chide farmers in such a pleasant way that instead of resenting the whip, they enjoy its application and ask for more. It's a gift.

*   *   *   *   *   *

Great exultation here this morning, for Messrs. Weatherby have written that as the gentleman who named his horse Farmer's Glory has gelded it and intends to use the animal for hunting, we can register our foal in this name. We have written to them forthwith to do this, and have formally christened the foal. His mistress says that he is to be called Farmer for short.

What will happen to him in years to come I cannot prophesy, for I cannot afford to have him trained, and am not capable of breaking him as a hunter. Most likely he will be sold as a yearling. But should any subsequent owner ever race him, no matter how little chance of winning he may appear to have, both Pam and I will invest a shilling or two on him every time he runs, just for old acquaintance' sake.

*   *   *   *   *   *

Our hopelessly old-fashioned and woefully mismanaged poultry department has been worrying me somewhat. A week or so ago, being in a gambling mood, I went to market with my wife and bought further additions to the stock, including, by way of a joke, six goslings.

Having had no previous dealings with either geese or goslings I imagined that this half dozen might provide some fun. Alas! Their purchase has proved a mistake; for as a result, instead of fun I have received nothing but scorn. Chickens and ducks are all right. The ladies of my household wait upon them, brag about them, and don't altogether enjoy seeing any of them on the table. But apparently goslings are different. They must possess that little something which other poultry hasn't got, for my wife and her companions in crime have all fallen in love with them.

The other day I besought my wife's help in the vetting of these notes. After all, it is a wise man who permits no written word to leave his house without first showing it to his better half. She may not know why something should be altered or deleted, but she always knows when it should be altered or deleted. At least, such is my fortunate experience.

But on this occasion my wife told me airily that she could not be bothered with me; because, forsooth, she must visit the goslings. To take second place to goslings in one's wife's affections seems to me to be a trifle hard. Dash it, had they been fully-grown geese it would not have hurt so much. But wait! Someday these young upstarts will be fully-grown, and then I shall get my own back.

* * * * * *

Is it my fancy, or is there really a little more money about this year? Anyway, just now there are two things connected with farming, which would seem to point out that such is the case. The former concerns game. During my journeying through the countryside I repeatedly come across a field covered with hen coops, each of which has a green bough laid in front of it to provide safe cover for young pheasant chicks. I am certain that there are many more acres of pheasant coops in England this summer, and I am very certain that each acre of them means a considerable sum of money.

The latter concerns horses. Horses of all kinds are very, very dear ; especially riding horses. Recently first-class hunters have made up to four hundred and thirty guineas at Tattersalls, and the three figure horse is a common occurrence. To give such high prices for hunters at this time of year, when they have to be turned out for three months, means that the buyer has faith in his or someone's financial future.

Which is all to the good for farming. Farmers may not be exactly rolling in money, but whenever the British townsman is doing well, much of his wealth (I nearly wrote illgotten) finds its way into the countryside.

Talking of horses, I have been rapidly coming to the conclusion that the keeping of riding horses is a vice. Even when the ground is hard and riding almost an impossibility, one cannot let one's nags alone. As time-wasters they are supreme. On the average I find myself spending at least one hour a day in daft conversation with my own horses. And when I compare such communion with the companionship of some human beings of my acquaintance I am forced to admit that horses win easily, heads down and tails swishing.

*   *   *   *   *   *

" Moderate or fresh northerly winds, with rain and hail, cool or very cool."

The above does not refer to the month of December,

but is a copy of the official weather forecast for all districts for Whitsun. Which just shows what the British climate can do when it feels like it.

Of course, farmers have a traditional right to grumble at the weather, but recently, and especially during the holiday week-end nearly everybody has copied our example. No one, not even a farmer, yearns for rain at holiday time, but really anything would have been preferable to what we have been having. This cold dry weather has been no good for anything ; no good for pleasure or for farming, which latter word, being translated, spells work. Warm rain would have been much more acceptable. It would have done no more harm to pleasuring, and such a lot of good to almost every branch of farming.

It occurs to me that just now is a kind of gap in country life. I don't mean a period in which there is no work, but rather one during which winter pleasures are out of season, and summer ones have not yet got going. We have said good-bye to hunting and shooting, but somehow it is difficult to raise much enthusiasm yet for fishing, tennis, or cricket. Very keen youth may be hard at work at the two latter pastimes, but sober middle-age is merely airing its flannels, and hoping for some hot weather. As a rule it is not until after hay-making that the farmer and his wife really get going with tennis.

But if sport and pleasure are at a standstill, work is not. On most farms it is all behind like the cow's tail, and long hours are being worked by men, horses, and machines in order to catch up with the date.

At this time of year especially does the early farmer catch the farming worm. In this part of England sugar-beet and mangolds have a much better chance of growing well when seed is sown during the last week in April ; and another advantage of early sowing is that the singling can be done before hay-making presses every hand into its service. The farmer, who in June is faced with a hundred acres of hay fit to mow and make and forty acres of sugar-beet and mangolds panicking to be singled, is usually an unhappy man. He lives for weeks between the devil of too-late cut hay and the deep sea of a weedy root field.

This year, I'm afraid, there will be a good many farmers in such a predicament, for the whole countryside seems to be at least two months behind. Hedgerows and woods are still bare and brown ; spring sown corn just refuses to make its appearance through the barren earth ; and the scene generally lacks the genial touch of spring. Apropos of the spring corn my old drowner said to me the other morning : " Don't 'ee worrit, zur. Long in bed, 'eavy at 'ead."

From his varied store of rhymes he can generally manage to find one which suits the mood of the moment in country matters ; and, more often than not, they tell the truth. But this year I have my doubts ; in May I prefer green oat fields to ones of barren brown.

And this year one of my aged friend's proverbs, " May never goes out without a wheat ear," does not fit at all. I can find no ears showing in my own wheat, and I have seen none anywhere in this district.

In summer, when the days are long,
Perhaps you'll understand this song——

Odds and Ends of Country Life

In spite of the cold, unseasonable weather, the country-side looks very lovely. Yesterday I drove almost due north from Salisbury as far as Leamington, and the May blossom lay like snow on the hedgerows every yard of the way. On this journey I was privileged to enjoy the company of my small-holder friend whom I have mentioned before. As it was his first visit to the grass country of the midlands he was very interested in the farming through which we drove, and I was none the less intrigued with his running commentary on everything and everybody we came across.

North of Oxford he was greatly concerned over two things—firstly, the apparent scarcity of stock in the fields; and secondly, the very wide grass verge on either side of the main road.

"Where be the cows?" he asked. "We've come a matter o' twenty mile since we lef' Oxford, an' I ain't seed more'n fifty all told."

I suggested that the country through which we were passing was noted more for beef than cows.

"Then where be the steers? Thee's know, they white-faced uns."

Here I pointed to a few Hereford cattle in a pasture near the road.

"Oh ah! There's mebbe 'alf a score calves there, but 'ow do 'em farm thease country wi'out stock. Damn it! There's on'y a vew sheep an' a 'andful o' cattle in grass land enough to carry thousands. Why down in Wil'shire we'd ha' zeed ten times as many."

I agreed, and suggested that the low prices for beef during recent years must have hit the grazing farmer so badly that he could no longer afford to stock his holding properly.

" Then he should get out, an' let zum other feller wot's properly briched 'ave a go," came the reply. " You cain't varm no land wi'out capital, an' you maun 'ave a zmartish vew aypence to stock good grass land as is vittin'."

While I agreed with this, I could not help thinking that the successful countryman's criticism of his unsuccessful neighbours is always more harsh than the townsman's ruling. Pursuing the same line of thought he proceeded to give me his real opinion of grazing as a method of farming.

" Thee's knaw," he said, " thic there grazin' job be a fool's game at the best o' times. 'Coorse, when there wur a li'l money to be got out o' it, it suited a lazy veller proper. But bless 'ee, when you kin make vive shillin' out o' grazin' you kin make fifteen out o' milk er breedin' young stock. But they capers do mane work. Ye zee, when you be a grazier, you do go to market to buy when you got zum grass, which be jist when every other vooil be at the zame game. An' when you do want to zell in the Fall when the grass be done, every other damn vooil be a zellin'. Consequent, you do git pinched zmartish both ways, which be on'y feasible."

All of which may or may not be quite fair comment, but it contains, I am sure, quite a lot of sound criticism of this method of farming. However, having exhausted this topic, he next turned his critical eye on the grass verges to the road.

" Why do 'em waste zo much ground, yerabouts ?" was his query. To which I replied that I imagined such wide grass verges had been left to enable the horseman to get along, seeing that we were travelling in a hunting country. As a horseman himself he could not altogether disagree with the procedure, but he stuck to it that the authorities had been far too lavish in the matter of grass verges.

" Reedicklus !" he said. " Why, a veller could cut a good rick o' hay every two mile. Still, zeein' as they cain't er wunt stock the grass tother side o' the 'edge, I 'low it don't matter about wastin' it along the road."

Coming homewards I suggested that we should have a cup of tea in Oxford.

" Ay, a cup o' tea 'ouldn' goo at all bad, I 'low an' should like fur to 'ave a look at thease yer Oxford. That be where they do taych young volk, bain't it ?"

Thinking that there was precious little Oxford teaching which my companion would value very highly, I pulled up outside a restaurant. We went inside, and ordered tea for two. When it came my companion eyed most suspiciously the plateful of cakes which the waitress had brought. They were of the cream puff and sugar topped varieties.

" H'm !" he said. " I doan't goo much on thic lot, missie. You be a good maid, an' bring along zum plain uns, plaze."

Whether the waitress was a good maid or not, she was highly amused at this form of address, and did his bidding in great good humour. While we ate, the restaurant filled up with customers, the majority of whom were young lads dressed in the popular uniform of modern youth—sports jacket and grey flannel slacks. My companion eyed them for some time, and then said, " Thease yer young chaps, they'll be studdin' at thease yer colleges, I 'low ?"

I told him that he had " 'lowed " correctly, whereupon in a voice which must have been heard by everyone in the room he said with great satisfaction, " Humph ! Then when I gits back 'ome, I shall be able to say that I bin to Oxford universe ?"

How wrong I was to think that Oxford held no message for my companion !

*   *   *   *   *   *

In my capacity of very fly fisherman I feel constrained to set down a few words of advice and caution to water keepers, secretaries, and other folk who are responsible for the upkeep of the fishing on our chalk streams. Naturally they do all they can to improve the fishing, but I would beg them to think well before they adopt some of the methods of improvement which have become so prevalent during recent years. In this matter they should take as their motto the line from Iolanthe, " As the ancient Romans said, ' Festina lente' " ; for otherwise they will spoil the fishing for the most appreciative fishermen—the very fly ones.

These crafty folk like to fish under natural conditions. They do not want every bush by the side of the river cut back, so that they can cast anywhere without let or hindrance. They enjoy creeping on their hands and knees, and losing several flies in vain attempts to switch just one Black Gnat to drop under that overhanging trail of bramble in the spot where the grandfather of all trout is rising steadily. They sometimes, nay often, curse the all-embracing meadow-sweet and other riverside plants which cause them to lose both fly and fish ; but they will curse more often, much louder, and much more venomously, when they find the bank trimmed like a formal garden.

It is a mistaken idea to imagine that these fishermen pay good money to fish a river from which all moorhens,

dabchicks, kingfishers, and even heron have been exterminated. They are well aware that the last-named does harm
to the fishing, but they prefer his occasional company to
the total lack of it. They do not continuously flog the
stream from dewy morn to bats and balmy eve. They have
no ambition to cover several miles of water in a day. They do
not want to fish a well-stocked tidy canal. They are very
fly fisherman.

What then do they want? First and foremost they want
to fish a natural river, on which they will be privileged to
watch the passing pageant of England's riverside birds and
beasts and reptiles pursuing their more of less lawful
avocations undisturbed. They do not curse when a flapping
moorhen puts a fish down. Instead they light a pipe, and
watch the river in placid content until their quarry regains
its confidence. For such connoisseurs the catching of fish
is merely one of the many pleasures of the day; the peace
and quiet and beauty and never-failing interest of their
surroundings count for far more.

Most fishermen rave about the Mayfly season, and say
that it provides them with a fortnight's perfect bliss. To
quote from an unreliable memory—

Jones would have told you that, or some such myth;
So would a hundred of his craft, and kith;
But I am Washington, where Jones and Smith
    Are liars.

My experience has been that the Mayfly season is often
very short and nearly always very disappointing; and I am
also regretfully aware that its conditions almost invariably
make even the very fly fisherman abandon his natural fishing
habit of peaceful sloth. Against his will he is forced to work
hard at his fishing; and, while once or twice in his life

Light a pipe and watch the river

during the Mayfly carnival he does fill his basket, more often than not he goes home tired, minus that blessed feeling of mental and physical content which a non-Mayfly day always bestows upon him.

It happens this way. The trout are rising everywhere. Each fish has dozens of flies passing over it every minute. In consequence, the chances of any particular fish taking the fisherman's fly are rather remote. But the rich plop of a rising fish spurs on the fisherman. After a quarter of an hour's casting at it, he hears the father of that fish rising with louder plops some twenty yards upstream. He moves up and starts work on father. In a few minutes grandfather fairly sploshes fifty yards downstream. Back goes the fisherman to try conclusions with him. Soon afterwards great-grandfathers, Abraham, Isaac, and Jacob, and many others disturb the face of the waters; and a bewildered but eager fisherman, no longer a very fly fisherman but a frantic, flailing man, continues his struggles until dark or exhaustion sends him home to beer and peace.

Such has been my experience with Mayfly, but to be fair I must confess that when they hatch out fairly slowly, and the weather is dull, this season can and does give most extraordinary sport and full baskets. It is almost impossible to forecast the exact date of the Mayfly season, but on Hampshire and Wiltshire streams the enthusiast should time his fishing holiday for the first fortnight in June. Most years, with any luck, during that period he should strike the Mayfly at their best.

But even if his luck be out he should not grumble. Rather should he give thanks; for now he will be able to become a very fly fisherman. He need not pack an elaborate variety of flies. March Brown, Blue Upright, Black Gnat, Alder, Red Spinner, and Wickham's Fancy will suffice; and with a supply of the first three only he can be assured of a good holiday. I have caught more trout with the March Brown and the Blue Upright throughout the season than with any other variety; and here be it noted that I, like most farmers, am a very bad fisherman, albeit very fly.

With such an outfit and without the excitements of the Mayfly the fisherman can meander slowly throughout the lovely deep blue day. By licence of the meadows and the river and the summer sun he will cease fishing repeatedly, and laze in contentment by the river's brim. A blue haze and a benign hush will enfold him during his after-luncheon nap, and when he wakes it will be to give thanks to the chalk stream and its surroundings for such natural luxury. Occasionally, very occasionally, he will meet a water-keeper,

He moves up

keeper, a drowner, or a dairyman; but none of these will disturb the serenity of his day, any conversation with them being of that satisfying sort—deep calling slowly to deep.

In between the enjoyment of these luscious delights he must, of course, do a little fishing. By careful stalking, quiet movement, and very little handling of his rod he may lure one or two trout to their doom, each successful cast being a work of art, carefully thought out and expertly accomplished. But with or without fish in his basket he will leave the river in the evening a very happy man. Why? Because he is a very fly fisherman.

*   *   *   *   *   *

Peter ended up the season very lame, and since then he has been turned out in a soft marsh with his shoes off, in the hope that the tinctures of time, rest, and soft going may make him sound once more. Glory is busy with her son and heir, and can spare no time for me; while Pam has laid it down that my weight is too much for Master Thomas Webster.

But I miss my daily ride, and feel sure that if I continue to miss it during the summer my weight will become too much for anything but a Suffolk Punch. So I have been thinking of buying another hack. Dash it! Up to date none of our riding horses has cost me a cent. Two were given to me, and Pam's cob is on loan. Surely I cannot be accused of being extravagant if I buy one nag for myself? So yesterday morning, finding myself at a loose end in town, I decided to visit Tattersalls for the first time in my life. Not that I had any thought of buying a horse there, but merely to spy out the land preparatory to future operations.

What a weird place that is to find in the heart of London! You emerge from the underground, and before you have walked fifty yards along the pavement you are forced to realize that London seems different somehow. The clop, clop of horses' hoofs sounds staccato against the hum and roar of the mechanical traffic. You look up to see some good hunters stepping gingerly as the grooms lead them between a bus and a taxi. You notice breeches and gaiters and even top boots along the pavements. One man passes you chewing a straw, and another slaps his leg with a riding whip as he gazes into the window of a famous store. It seems as though the scents of brake and coppice are wafted through the petrol fumes; and suddenly London seems very far away.

Tattersalls

At least, that was how it seemed to me the other morning when I left Knightsbridge station, and when I entered the premises it seemed more so. The main business carried on there would seem to be the selling of horses, but I could not help noticing some other features. One was that I was dressed all wrong. At Tattersalls you should wear a bowler hat, preferably one of small size. Never have I seen so many of these gathered together in one place, and my rather shabby felt stamped me as a novice from the word go.

In addition the rest of my attire left much to be desired. I was surrounded by breeches or very narrow trousers, stocks, fancy waistcoats, and such clever faces. Even the ladies present looked as though they knew all about horses ; and so I, who realized my limitations in this respect as well as in my dress, crept through this forest of masculine nutshell bowlers and determined feminine chins in most humble fashion.

Tattersalls is almost unique in another respect, I should imagine, for it is one of the few places in town to-day, always excepting places of worship, where smoking is most strictly prohibited. Indeed, it might well be termed a place of worship, the worship of the horse, and those who would worship at this shrine must be content to keep their tobacco in their pockets the while. Some of the horses there are worthy of worship, too ; and, as the prices they fetch show, some people are ready to pay handsomely for their religion. Such an expensive outward and visible sign of belief is denied me ; but I did find that rich and poor and male and female in the congregation that morning had one thing in common. Indeed, in this particular connection, I, in spite of my trilby hat and wideish trousers, was equal to anyone present.

Sometimes a horse flourished its heels as it was being

run up and down, whereupon the worshippers who crowded near the altar retired in haste from their idol's displeasure. And so did I. One touch of nature makes the whole world kin.

So fascinated was I with the whole place that before I realized it the time was one-thirty ; and, as I had an appointment in Fleet Street an hour later, a proper lunch was out of the question. In search of some sandwiches I wandered into a pub near by, and there again a truly rural flavour greeted me.

The place was packed with countryfolk, and for a moment I thought I had been suddenly transported back to the Blue Lion down in Wilts on market day. I bagged some ham sandwiches and a glass of beer, and sat down to feed and listen. I heard that one horse had " never bin knowed to turn 'is 'ead at nothin'," that another was not only a pig but " stinkin' dear," and that when it came to an aged horse making over three hundred guineas one of my companions was of opinion that the purchaser "wanted his head seen to."

Then just before I left I saw a man who had a fox cub seated on his shoulder. It was quite tame ; and, although it drank from its owner's glass in most dainty fashion, quite convinced that Guinness was good for it.

Never did an appointment in Fleet Street seem less attractive.

*   *   *   *   *   *

Fifty years ago it was a generally accepted axiom that a young man would prefer to have his morals doubted rather than his knowledge of horseflesh. Presumably a similar preference obtains to-day with regard to his morals and motor cars ; for, while every young man must know all about superchargers or be considered a poor fish by his fellows and his girls, I doubt whether his valuation of his morals has changed very much, if at all.

However, as a friend of mine says at the bridge table when some reckless bidding he lays down a hopelessly inadequate dummy, " it's nothing to do with me." A young man's morals and his knowledge of either cars or horses cannot be my concern, for it is a regrettably long time since I could be described as a young man. It is my own knowledge of horseflesh or lack of it which has been worrying me ; for I want to buy a horse.

To buy a new car is a simple matter, provided you have the wherewithal, and apparently even if you haven't. To buy a horse is much more difficult, being fraught with danger from the word go. There is, I admit, a certain similarity between buying a horse and a second-hand car, in that there is usually an if or a but about the ultimate purchase ; but there the resemblance ends. Even in the second-hand car market the paying of a high price usually ensures an efficient vehicle, and at any rate one which can be repaired and fitted with new parts if necessary. In contrast, the good horse may cost a fiver, and the hopeless " wrong un " may cost three figures ; and neither can be fitted with new parts Another difficulty is that the animal which is a good horse to one man, may be a snare and a delusion to another. For instance, while it is comparatively easy to drive the super-charged car at a reasonable speed, to control the super-charged horse is often difficult, sometimes impossible, and for me much too nerve-wracking.

My own particular trouble is that I am so much heavier than my pocket. I do not want a young horse, I do not want a fast horse, but I do want a cheap, quiet horse which can carry my fifteen stone ; and already I have discovered that cheapness and weight-carrying do not go together, especially if they have to be allied with perfect manners and the ability to hop over a hurdle on occasion. What I really want is an old police horse. For years I have coveted such a horse. Think of it—a horse which would not flinch even though a salvo of guns was fired under his nose ; a horse which would stand immovable what time the music from several brass bands went round and around him—Peter and I once met a brass band, and only the mercy of providence kept us together ; a horse which could both stop and go, but only when I so desired ; a horse well up to my weight, sound as a bell, a good looker, a comfortable ride, and, of course, cheap. But alas, old police horses never seem to come into the market. What happens to them I don't know, but I have a shrewd notion that they end their days on government pension, and beguile their well-earned leisure by writing detective stories.

So I have acted on the maxims laid down for me by my late father, all of which have been proved correct by some twenty odd years of farming experience. " Live and let live," " better the devil you know than the devil you don't," and " in order to buy well learn to be a judge of your fellow men," were three that I obeyed. I have been to the devil I know, that very good dealer friend who sold me Pam's first pony, and stated my requirements.

He grinned, and suggested that I did not want much for my money. " A 'oss such as you says you wants, everybody in England do want," he said. " An' 'ee'd be dirt cheap at two 'underd quid. But you don't want a good 'oss at all. Fur one thing you ain't got the job fur 'im an' fur another you bain't up to it. You wants a useful plug, wot can 'ack 'ee safe, an' let 'ee see the 'ounds once in a way when

Miss Pam's 'ome from school. You lave it to me."

Feeling rather squashed, I inquired what sort of money such a useful plug would be.

" You do niver know," he said oracularly. " Ee'll ha' to be found, an' 't'ull 'ave to be a sensible sort of an 'oss to carry you, fur you be got tarblish stout. But I shain't 'urt 'ee ; you do know that well enough. Still, 'osses be dear, so you'd best try round on yer own, jist fur eddication."

And with this advice I came away.

*   *   *   *   *   *

In obedience to my friend's advice I have been trying to find a horse on my own hook ; not that I doubt his capabilities to produce the right animal at the right price, but in order to show him that I can sometimes do things without his aid. But I have found this quest a nerve-wracking and wearing business. Having acquired two horses for nothing through the medium of the private owner's advertisement, I have been answering dozens of these and journeying far and wide to try the goods so advertised which took my fancy. But to-day's adventure has decided me to abandon this form of search. As my friend and adviser put it in connection with my buying a good horse, " I bain't up to it."

This morning's animal seemed to be just the mount for me. He was described as being seventeen hands, up to weight, quiet, a good jumper, and sound save for a slight noise which was not supposed to stop him. I clambered on to his back, and he walked off down the road like a gentleman. But when he found some turf under his feet. Whew! He not only made a noise, he made me wish I was anywhere but on his back. Thank goodness, I tried him on a Monday morning, for only the washing on the line prevented him from jumping a six foot paling into somebody's garden. He was, I suppose, everything his owner said about him, but I knew my limitations. So I have decided to go to fountain head; and next Monday I shall go up to Tattersalls.

* * * * * *

A barren cold May and continued dry cold during the beginning of June has resulted in a very light hay cut in this district ; and now comes the question—to get on with hay-making, in the hope of achieving a " little and good " result, or to wait awhile, in the hope that copious warm rain will soon fall ? Last year, to my regret, I took the former course, and the rain came in early June just after I had downed sixty acres of grass. So I shall give it just two more days, and then begin cutting, on the assumption that very rarely indeed do we get the same weather two years in succession.

Indeed, no matter what the weather I am convinced that it pays to cut grass early, for when one leaves it standing until it gets old the resultant hay is never of very good feeding value. Also, when grass is cut young, it will stand a lot of rain without deteriorating in quality very much. Some of my last year's early cut hay, which stayed in swath under continuous rain until the aftermath grew up and completely hid it from sight, gave a better flow of milk than some late cut stuff which was made without one spot of wet.

* * * * * *

Rarely do I journey to London, except on business connected with writing or broadcasting, certainly not more than once a year entirely on pleasure bent. But yesterday I went up solely for my own pleasure ; that is to say, to buy a cheap but quiet and sound horse.

I mapped out my plan of campaign in the train, and

decided that if I followed it I could not go wrong. Let the young and the wealthy have the fast young horses and pay the price, I thought. Here is where indigent middle-age shall be content with an aged horse of good character for a very few guineas. So, in the midst of a crowd of clever faces surmounted by smallish bowler hats, I, a poor scribbler whose rather innocent countenance was topped with but a battered trilby, wandered through the stables. I saw horses old and horses young, horses short and horses tall, horses with good characters and horses with none, and horses of every shape and colour imaginable.

With great care I selected two horses, one on the groom's recommendation, and the other because I liked everything about him. The first was admitted to be thirteen years old, and to be so quiet and capable that his owner during the last years of his life, although he had to be lifted on to him, could go like a bird in Leicestershire. Such a paragon would just about suit me, I decided, and surely a thirteen year old horse would be within reach of my pocket. The second was a twelve-year-old chestnut which I could not fault, no matter how much I tried; and his genuine friendliness to a stranger caused me to fall in love with him. If I do not get the first at my limit of fifty guineas, I thought I will buy this horse, even if he does make a trifle more. After all, I shall be paying only one more guinea than the previous bidder's valuation.

But somehow I did not buy either of my selections. The first made one hundred and eighty guineas, and the second over three hundred. I may not be a young man; my morals may not be all they should be; but, after this, no one can question my taste in horseflesh.

*   *   *   *   *   *

Feeling in a somewhat chastened mood after my fruitless search for the right horse at the right price, I have abandoned the struggle, and decided to leave it to my dealer friend's convenience to produce the "useful plug" according to his promise. Meantime I have been helping Pam in the education of both Farmer and Thomas Webster. The former is fast learning to enjoy his evening haltering and subsequent parade, and the latter is being schooled over jumps.

Thomas likes jumping, but he definitely does not agree with the girl who said that she was game to try anything once. Master Tom takes the opposite view. He is quite game to try some things—jumps which he knows—as many times as his mistress wishes. He cocks his eye at them, gives a little chuckle as if to say, " This is all right. Come on, let's go," and sails over in great style. But anything new to him he views with grave suspicion. Hurdles are definitely his meat, and the double jump composed of hurdles he treats with lissome contempt. But when first introduced to a low brush jump, only half as high as a hurdle, he stuck his toes in and slid ungracefully through it.

Resuming afresh, he proceeded to jump nearly five feet in his endeavours to avoid prickles some two feet high. Thank goodness, Pam and he were still together when he came down on the other side. However, after repeated trials and approbations, he has decided that brush jumps are O.K., and jumps them very prettily. I have promised, when I have time, to erect a white painted triple bar, and possibly an imitation wall so that he shall make his bow to these strange things in private and not before the critical gaze of a gymkhana audience. But I doubt whether this will get done before haymaking is finished, for we downed twenty acres of grass yesterday.

This afternoon I spent an entertaining hour with a neighbour and his men who were busy gassing rats in and around his farm buildings. An old car with some fifty yards of hosepipe attached to its exhaust pipe formed the equipment, and very efficient it was.

A few seconds after the end of the hosepipe had been stuffed a foot or so down a rat hole, things happened. I should imagine that the majority of rats bolt when they smell the gas, for we had an exciting time killing some thirty or forty with sticks. Incidentally, farm labourers get so excited when a rat is running between their feet that it is advisable to wear stout boots, and to insist that all sticks shall be on the short side—thirty inches long is ample. But in one instance we dug out half a dozen dead rats in a blind end of a burrow, which must have been killed very quickly by the exhaust fumes.

I understand that this method can be used on rabbits with some success, but that for this class of vermin some form of Calcium Cyanide, introduced into the burrows in powder form by means of a blower, is the better method. There is, my friend told me, some little apprehension amongst farm labourers about handling such a deadly poison ; but he added that most of the firms who supply it are prepared to make the first " drive " over the ground with their own experts, during which operation they will instruct one of the farm hands in the proper use of their tackle. He also said that once this has been done the average farm worker, with the usual gumption of the countryman, finds it easy to carry on efficiently without expert assistance. This I can well believe.

Well, the gassing of my rabbits, either by car or blower, is another job which must be deferred until the haymaking has been successfully tackled.

*　　*　　*　　*　　*　　*

My dealer friend arrived yesterday in time for tea with the news that the " useful plug " had been found. " Not much to look at," he said, " but 'ee'll do your job proper."

" What sort o' wages ?" I inquired, whereupon he grinned widely. " A zmartish bit cheaper than they 'osses as you didn' buy up Lunnon," he chuckled.

" How the devil do you know that I've been up to Tattersalls ?" I said in amazement.

" Aw ! I do knaw well enough. Ye see, 'tis me bizness to knaw thic zort o' thing. Bill Brewer wur up there thic day, an' he telled me all about yer doin's."

Thank goodness I don't live in Devon ; otherwise in addition to Bill Brewer, I should have " Jan Stewer, Peter Davey, Peter Gurney, 'Arry 'Awk, and Uncle Tom Cobley an' all " keeping watch on my activities. Feeling very crestfallen I related my exploits in town and bragged of my good taste in horseflesh.

" Jist zo ! But they 'osses as you picked out wur Leicestershire 'osses. You don't want a Leicestershire 'oss down in thease country. There bain't nothin' for'n to do. An' *you* don't want nothin' very special at all. Thease 'oss as I've a voun' ull do thy job proper, an' he'm gwaine to cost 'ee 'bout twenty-vive poun'."

Twenty five pounds seemed an extraordinarily low figure for a horse which could make any attempt at carrying me, so I inquired particulars.

" He'm at B———, matter o' twenty mile. Young So-and-so, thee's know, 'im wot do win the pint-to-pints, 'ee've jist got un back vrom the Yeomanry, where 'ee bin on 'ire. 'Ee telled I as the 'oss wur main poor, but a good sensible 'oss. Thee drive I down atter tea, an' 'ave a look at 'n.''

After tea we set out, to be told by the horse's owner when we arrived that the animal was turned out in a water-meadow about half a mile away. So the three of us walked off to have a look at him. On our way we passed a gentle-man busy fishing a large hatch pool.

" Salmon ?'' I asked the farmer.

" Yes ! That's supposed to be the best pool south o' Scotland,'' he said. " Gosh ! An' don't they pay for it ? This fishing works out at about twenty-five guineas per rod per day.''

Now anything which has money in it holds a message for our dealer friend, and at this remark he metaphorically sat up and took notice of this fishing business. First of all he wanted to know just who captured these fabulous sums of money which foolish sportsmen paid so willingly.

" I don't 'low,'' he ventured, " that thease fishin' be throwed in wi' the farm.''

" Good heavens, no,'' said the farmer. " If 'twas, I could have retired ten year back. I rent the land for farmin', the fishin's reserved.''

" Zim a daftish caper, wavin' thic hrod about all day,'' the dealer opined. " Do 'em iver ketch any ? 'Ouldn' it be aisier to net 'em ?''

" I've known that gentleman catch eight of a day,'' answered the farmer. " That's young Lord So-and-so.''

Twenty-five guineas per day and aristocracy combined were so attractive to our companion, that he left the path we were following, and walked over to the fisherman. The

farmer and I continued on our way, but we were near
enough to hear the following conversation.

" Avenin' !"

" Good evening.   Warmer to-night isn't it ?"

" Ay !   Ketched arn ?"

What the fisherman replied I know not, for our steps had
taken us out of earshot, but I am convinced that we missed
many more such gems of conversation. Five minutes later our
friend rejoined us with, " That bain't sich a vooil game as
I thought. Thic veller've ketched vower. Average nigh
on twelve poun' apiece. Wot be zammon wuth a poun'
thease time o' year ?"

" God knows," answered the farmer, whilst I forgot my
manners sufficiently to yelp my delight aloud. " But
there's the 'oss. Poor as a rook, but he's sound, and he'll
doddle Mr. Street about proper, an' when he'm in condition,
I tell 'ee that's no fool out huntin'."

How true it is that one cannot fool one's country neighbours ! But I do wish that they were blessed with a little
more tact. I do want a horse to "doddle" me about, and I
know that they know that I want that type of animal ; but
I don't exactly relish hearing this stated aloud. However,
in spite of the horse's poor condition, and generally plain
appearance, I have promised to come down another evening
when he will be in stable and I shall be able to throw a leg
over him.

At least, that was how we put it, but in my case the word
" throw " gives an entirely false impression of my methods.

*   *   *   *   *   *

A neighbour told me something this morning, which
illustrates the difference in attitude of townsman and
countryman to rabbits. To the former they are such

charming little animals ; to the latter they are such destructive vermin.

Driving home late the other night with his wife, as their car was passing along a narrow lane which was roofed overhead by arched trees and bordered on either side by steep banks, they saw in the glare of the headlights four rabbits, running furiously away. My friend slowed down to about fifteen miles per hour, but still the rabbits continued their marathon.

" Poor little beggars," he said to his wife. " We must have driven 'em a good mile from home already. They'll die of heart disease in a minute. I'd better stop."

This he did, whereupon the rabbits did likewise, and sat upon their haunches in the glare, twiddling their whiskers quite happily. So he switched out his lights, and the green tunnel through which they had been driving suddenly seemed very dark.

After a few moments' patient waiting they saw the gleam of one rabbit's eyes, as he came back to inspect the silent car. Finding all safe, he ran back to tell his companions, and a few moments later all four crept back, passed the car, and presumably set off for home.

* * * * * *

For better or worse, I have purchased the aforementioned horse for the sum of twenty guineas, a sentence which appears to be a cross between the marriage service and a legal document. This evening, I drove down with my mentor and performed the feat of leg-throwing, which appeared so necessary. The horse proved to be quiet, apparently sound, and blessed with a snaffle mouth. But he was slow, and being a black, one thought of funerals.

Those two clever devils, my companions, watched my

what did I expect for £5 a Derby Winner?

progress and waited for my comments in blank silence. The one had a horse to sell, the other had discovered the said horse, and if I bought him both were going to touch money. The delights of friendship were all very well up to a point, but it was very evident that the point had been reached when these satisfying things must give way to strict business. Hence their silence and non-committal expressions. It was up to me.

Well, I had to say something, so I said that the horse was too slow, whereupon my dealer friend said, " 'Ee'm vast enough for you."

This nettled me. Blast it! Did they think I had arrived already at the donkey and bath chair time of life? So I said that the horse wasn't much to look at, which was true. Dash it, I thought, I may not be a good horseman, but I do want a nag to enable me to look the part.

This criticism was encountered on the one part by a growl that " 'andsome was as 'andsome did," and on the other by a eulogy of the horse's looks and capabilities what time he had had sufficient grub stuffed into him. So I said that he was too dear, and then we got to it. What did I expect for twenty-five pounds? A Derby winner? What about the old horses at Tattersalls which I had vainly imagined I could buy? What in the name of fortune was twenty-five quid, anyway? So then I produced an argument which reduced both my companions to a bewildered silence, and almost to tears.

"You don't understand," I said. "The last two horses I got cost me nothing. They were given to me. That makes this horse look stinkin' dear."

Never have I triumphed so splendidly over two such clever countrymen, and once again I record my thanks to that lady who presented me with Peter and Glory.   My two companions tried to argue that gift horses did not count, but they put up a very poor show.   Still, I expect the real financial triumph was theirs, for I bought the nag, and he is coming home by lorry to-morrow.

And now for haymaking !

*   *   *   *   *   *

"Flies !"

Haytime

I well remember my father telling me that each year in my life would bring weather different from anything which I had previously experienced. Well, this one is no exception to his rule ; for a few days ago I saw something in a Wiltshire hayfield which I had never seen before. It was this— a carter driving two horses hitched to a mowing machine, and walking behind the cutter in order to keep warm ! ! I have walked many hundreds of miles behind a sleigh over a snow trail in north-west Manitoba for the same reason ; but, in this country, for a man to be compelled to walk behind a grass mower in June !

Wheat does not seem to be very happy with the weather this season, for I have yet to see what I should call a good field. This cereal is supposed to enjoy a wet winter and a sweltering summer. The former happened all right, possibly a trifle too much so ; but the latter has not yet put in an appearance. I have only a very small wheat field this year —just three acres for thatch put into an odd corner of arable after sugar beet. It looks fairish, but I don't anticipate a very heavy yield.

Talking of sugar beet, there does not seem to be many acres of this crop in Wiltshire this season. No matter what some folk think should be the driving force behind man's work in this world, in farming and in every other industry it is the hope of reward that sweetens labour. Consequently in counties where the carriage rate to the nearest sugar factory destroys all hope of reward from the growing of

Grass mower at work

sugar beet, there is very little grown. I should imagine that the acreage of sugar beet in Wiltshire is down 50 per cent. on last year's.

But where mangolds are grown in the county there seems to be a good regular plant. On June 2nd I saw a field already singled, and out of harm's way, which is as early as I have ever known.

And what a change has taken place in the amount of grass keep available. On May 25th there was an ample supply. On June 1st the cows were bawling, and on some farms they had to be turned into a field which had been laid up for hay. Nothing shrinks grass in summertime more quickly than dry weather coupled with a north-east wind.

*　　　*　　　*　　　*　　　*　　　*

As soon as I had some eighty acres of grass cut, down came the rain, so I cried " Halt " to the mower, thinking that this acreage was more than sufficient hostage to fortune.

So for two or three days we have been doing some fencing jobs, and waiting the weather's pleasure.

This season I have been using a trailer mower behind a tractor, having sold my power-drive mower with the old tractor ; and I do not regret the change. Here let me hasten to say that I have nothing but praise for the power-drive mower. Properly used it is a most excellent tool, but it possesses one feature which tends to make it a good tool badly handled in the majority of cases.

For some years now I have noticed that the carter with two horses and an ancient mower almost invariably did better work than the tractor driver with a tractor and brand new power-drive mower ; and these last few wet days I have driven about the countryside confirming this and seeking for an explanation. Conversations with neighbours and my own experience this season with a trailer mower has provided what I consider to be a feasible one. No grass mower will make a decent job with a blunt knife. True, any fool knows that ; but when any fool, or even someone who is by no means a fool, is given a twenty horse-power engine to drive the knife of his mower backwards and forwards, he is tempted to neglect his knife sharpening. On the other hand, the carter, no matter how much he might wish to dodge this tiresome job, is forced to keep his knife sharp, because otherwise he cannot get his horses along ; and even the tractor driver with a trailer mower is compelled to do so. There is no doubt in my mind that where a farmer uses a power-drive mower he should always send two men with it, one to drive and the other to sharpen knives. When this is done the power-drive does a perfect job.

*   *   *   *   *   *

Managed to snaffle twenty acres of hay to-day in not too bad condition, and once again I gave thanks for the rapid efficiency of the car-sweep. Although he dislikes most new implements the farm labourer has nothing but praise for this one. By comparison with either the horse-sweep or the tractor variety its method of " little and often " means much easier work for the men who have to pitch the hay into the elevator ; a big sweep load means that they have to " sweat their guts out " pulling it apart. But to-day the drowner gave me the real reason why the car-sweep has become so popular with British farmers.

" Ay ! That be a good tool," he opined, when we were stopped for tea. " Tell 'ee fur why. You farmers be a lazy lot, the main on 'ee. Take yerself now, you doan't like work, do 'ee ? Real 'ard work, I mean ?"

" True, Jim," I admitted. After all, it was useless to attempt to conceal my true character from a man who had watched my career from babyhood.

" Jist zo. But you doan't mind a settin' at yer ease in a motycar, a buzzin' atheart an' across the vield, an' doin' the work o' zix men an' four 'osses, comfortable like. Jist your clip, that be. I tell 'ee they car-sweeps 'ave put more farmers to work in their own 'ayfields than ever bad times 'ave."

And the more I think about it, the more I am convinced that Jim has the rights of it. Driving horses in a hayfield is a slow job, and the flies bite you all the time ; driving a tractor is a trifle quicker, but it is a very dirty business, and soon results in your clothes and even your skin reeking of paraffin ; but to sit at one's ease on a comfortable leather car seat and to know that one is doing a lot of good work is good enough for me and for most farmers.

I do not think that many townsfolk have any notion of how mechanically-minded our rural population has become during recent years. Haymaking is perhaps an especially mechanized branch of farming, and during the next few weeks rural England will be swarming with machines from dawn till dark ; but at every season of the year the farm labourer is using machinery daily. In fact, I think generally that he possesses a much greater knowledge of cars and internal combustion engines than his town cousin. So many townsfolk use these inventions, but have no intimate knowledge of their working. They buy their ticket, and are transported to their destination ; but most farm labourers drive and tend a car, lorry, tractor, or engine every working day of their lives.

During haymaking everybody on the farm is a chauffeur of sorts. I have seen twelve-year-olds driving high-powered hay-sweep cars in the hayfield with surprising dexterity and rather terrifying nonchalance ; for this familiarity at such a tender age soon breeds a rather dangerous contempt. Still, perhaps by the time these lads reach the age when they can drive on the highway the dangerous novelty of mechanical transport will have worn off into safe boredom.

Of course, hand in hand with the rapid increase of mechanization on our farms there has been a corresponding decrease in the number of work-horses. Indeed, on many farms in the south of England the carthorse is becoming conspicuous by its absence. For instance, I have but one carthorse on a farm of three hundred and twenty acres ; which lives out of doors with the cows, and has not tasted an oat or slept in a stable for the past six years. In spite of this he is always as fat as a pig, and I doubt whether he does fifty days' work in a year.

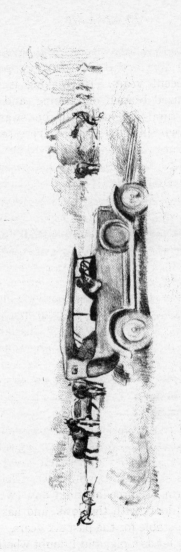

a horseman without a head

But if work-horses are disappearing from both town and country life the play-horses are coming back ; for more and more people of both sexes, and of all ages are learning to ride. Which is queer. Why should people, who own cars which can transport them in comfort at fifty miles per hour, prefer to spend their leisure in being shaken about on the back of a horse at about one fifth of that speed ? Apart from the slowness, imagine the popularity of a car which possessed a similar gait.

This change in our habits is hardly logical ; it is, in reality, a revolt against the domination of the machine. We have become so sick and tired of mechanical work, that during our leisure we yearn to play with something alive. Of course, if townspeople wish to ride, countryfolk must breed riding horses. This they are doing, for once again demand has created supply. Farmers who have almost abandoned the use of carthorses in their business are now breeding light horses, and many more mares and foals can be found in English pastures this summer.

*   *   *   *   *   *

A bad thunderstorm last night, which has put paid to any further haymaking for a few days, and possibly longer, I write that because although I cannot quite agree with my men that rain " breeds " thunder, I have often noticed that thunder upsets the weather and leaves it unsettled for some time.

I got up early this morning as I was rather worried about Farmer being out in the paddock with his mother during the storm. People who make a business of breeding thoroughbreds usually get their mares and foals in stable during summer nights for fear of them being frightened by thunderstorms, and those who perhaps do not do this fence their paddocks with high wood palings which are painted white. Our paddock is a purely utilitarian one from a cow-farming angle, and is therefore fenced with barbed wire, that good fence for cows, and such a dangerous one for horses.

The little man whickered when he saw me, and came trotting across the paddock to say, "Good morning." He had evidently run into the wire once, for his nose had a slight prick, and there was a little jag on his chest. I got some iodine and some moist sugar, the former for his wounds, and the latter to comfort his soul, or possibly his tummy. Then, I rather shamefacedly reported the matter to his owner. Greatly concerned she visited the patient while arrayed in pyjamas and dressing gown ; of course, at the time all unbeknown to her mother. Result—two edicts have gone forth. One, that Glory and Farmer are to be housed nightly until the thundery weather has disappeared ; and two, that even owners of thoroughbreds must dress properly before they visit their blood stock.

*   *   *   *   *   *

Three days comparative farming inactivity, and then the weather cleared up. In consequence, there does not seem to be much to write about this week save haymaking, and very certainly there has been little opportunity to sit down at a desk. Recently my life and the lives of most farmers have been ruled by haymaking ; for all forms of pleasure have to be abandoned and all other branches of the farm's activities must play second fiddle when a June sun is flaming over the fields. In fact, by comparison with the feverish rush of haymaking, the corn harvest becomes just a pleasant and rather leisurely business.

Indeed, one of my neighbours described haymaking to

me the other day as the " curse of farming." " Think of
it," he said. " You worry through the winter, you get
your crops planted in the spring, and just when some nice
weather comes along and you might enjoy life a little, you
have to contend with the harassing business of haymaking."

When I pointed out that modern implements made
haymaking a much easier business than formerly, he fairly
blew up. " Do they ?" he snarled. " Yes and no. Their
use means that you can shift more hay per man employed,
but also that the master's worries have increased tremendously. Machinery has a nasty habit of breaking down,
usually of course just when you have a large field of hay fit
to rick. Our grandfather's haymaking must have been
peace perfect peace compared with ours. They had about
forty men in the field ; we have six men and sixty complicated contraptions. I tell you that after a day's haymaking
in which everything has gone wrong, I'm a pretty heavy
cross for my wife and family to bear. In fact, I'm not fit
society for anybody."

When he said this I was immediately conscious that I
was far from guiltless in this respect, and I know that most
of my neighbours would be forced to say the same. It is
the chancy nature of haymaking which is so annoying. In
a catchy season it is possible to make no good hay or all
good hay, according whether your luck is in or out in the
timing of the cutting of each field. Besides, the damage
done by a thunderstorm to a field of good hay which is fit
to carry is ten times what the same storm would do to a
field of corn in similar condition.

It is this annual worry connected with haymaking which
is one of the reasons for the keen interest which so many

Machinery has a nasty habit of cracking down

farmers are taking in this grass drying business. " When that job becomes a business proposition for the average farm," said one of my friends to me the other day, " I shall throw up my hat. Think of it. A little steady grass cutting and drying day after day from May until September. No rush, no worries, no blasted haymaking. When that happens, my boy, farming will be a gentleman's life."

" Well, what is it now ?" I asked.

He grinned. " Hell on earth during haymaking, and no so bad for the rest of the year," he said.

Whereupon, as this conversation took place in the lane by the side of my own hayfield, and he was on his way home with a spare part for a mower, I could not resist saying, " Well then, you'd better go to hell, for that's where I'm off to. Just look at that sun."

But every calling has its particular drawbacks and advantages, and I can never see that farming has more than its share of the former. It is easy to grouse about the weather during one particular season, but any farmer who reviews the effects of weather on his farming during a period of ten years will be bound to confess that the British climate has dealt very fairly with him. Besides, all the talk about the countryman being compelled to work outdoors in all winds and weathers is just so much ballyhoo. I pity the poor folk who are forced to work indoors all the year round. Haymaking under a June sun is a preferable job to indoor work in most large towns.

And think of the journey home after work is done. I once travelled in the underground just after six p.m. from Piccadilly Circus to Hounslow. It was a hot July evening, the coach was crowded, and I stood all the way. Once was enough for me, but most of my companions do that journey

Haytime

every day, both night and morning. How they stand it I cannot imagine. A week of it would finish me.

Last night I came home in an old hay-sweep car. I grant that it was so packed with haymakers that some of us were sitting on the others' laps, but what of that? Compared with that underground journey it was the height of comfort.

*　　*　　*　　*　　*　　*

It is many years since I enjoyed a tankard of beer so much as I did this morning. It was one of those mornings when if I had stayed at home I should have carried some hay which was not quite fit—any farmer will understand the position; so I removed myself from temptation by going for a ride on the useful plug, now christened Blackbird. The day was pure gold, and the countryside a glory all the way. So pleasant was the journey that I continued it for ten miles, and called upon my dealer friend.

He wanted to show me two pony colts, and suggested that I should put my horse in his stable, and ride down to the pasture in his governess cart. Suddenly realizing that I had not ridden in such a vehicle for nearly twenty years I agreed, and, with my friend's small grand-daughter to make up the party, away we went.

As we spanked through the village I suddenly found myself back in pre-war days. I sat forward as the cob breasted a slope, and sat back as he clattered down the other side; my friend shouted greetings to everyone we passed; and I felt on top of the world.

On the way back as we passed the village pub I suddenly remembered that I was thirsty—after all a ten mile hack under a June sun was a reasonable excuse. I pointed this out to our whip, whereupon he swung the trap in a fine

Dreamt myself back in pre war days

semi-circle to the door of the inn. In a few minutes the landlord brought our drinks, lemonade for the lady and beer for the gentlemen.

And that is the proper setting in which to drink beer—in the sunshine at the door of a village inn, with a pony and trap outside, a few cocks and hens scratching around you, and the ripe discourse of two countrymen to flavour the beverage. For a few moments I was living in my world of twenty years ago, in a countryside which had not been raped by the internal combustion engine, in a social scheme in which there was no need to hurry. It was gorgeous.

In contrast my hayfield this evening was one mechanical buzz, during which I became more than ever convinced that the real value of the countryside to England is that it does enable a few folk, such as my drinking friends of the morning, to avoid the mechanical maelstrom of modern civilization. In these days when most of us live such peripatetic lives we should be badly off without the solid background of a few rural folk who " stay put."

*   *   *   *   *   *

It occurs to me that I have neglected Blackbird in this notebook since his arrival ; but really, he was so thin that he needed food far more than exercise, and I have been so busy haymaking that I have had no time to ride him very much. Still, I have had him for over a fortnight now, and, although I could wish that he had a trifle more go in him, as yet I can find no flaw. Almost I am beginning to think that he is cheap ; which, as Euclid said about many things which are much less attractive than horses, is absurd.

Still, he does enable me to go pottering through the countryside into places which the car cannot reach, and for this boon I am very grateful. I often think that a farming life is like fishing in that unless one is content with the natural things on offer both lose their charm. If a man expects to farm, and to enjoy all the incidental and inexpensive pleasures which can be a part of this calling, together with all the amenities and delights of town, he will almost invariably come a mucker. The land will not provide and should not be expected to provide both varieties. For instance, that ride of mine the other morning, with its accompanying delights which I have mentioned—what would not many townsmen pay to enjoy such a morning ? And having written that I must go to bed, after first confessing that I am going to town next Monday and next Saturday. But man was never a logical animal.

*   *   *   *   *   *

We have snaffled a hundred acres of hay not too badly at all considering the weather, and the remainder, although it comprises some thirty acres in all, might fairly be termed trimmings. These will be well worth stacking, but we have broken the back of our annual worry. So to-day, as it was Pam's half-term holiday, I fulfilled an old-standing promise to drive my household to London. We left first thing after breakfast in brilliant sunshine, and arrived at the " Wives' Paradise and Husbands' Despair " at ten a.m. ; which, of course means Knightsbridge, for the Summer Sales began to-day.

I bore with my womenfolk until one o'clock, when I insisted on lunch. During the meal I deliberately tempted Pam by telling her that Tattersalls was only just across the road. Her own wardrobe having been restocked during the forenoon, she fell for it ; and so, leaving my wife and my niece to carry on the search for bargains, we escaped further sale tortures during the afternoon.

What the future holds for my daughter, goodness only knows, but at the moment horses are her major interest. She loved every minute of the afternoon, and voted Tattersalls the best place in London she had ever visited. She watched a very little girl's excited and anxious face while her father was bidding for a pony. She fairly worshipped one old gentleman who wore such tight trousers and such a glorious stock and pin. She gazed with awe at the horses which topped the three-figure mark. She inspected the antique coaches and other vehicles in the gallery upstairs, and sat there, almost directly above the auctioneer's box, while some twenty light draught horses belonging to a famous whisky firm were being sold. She valued each horse during its first run towards the box, and made me do the same, exulting when her judgment proved better than mine—a thing which happened many more times than I had anticipated. And, in common with most folk present, she mourned aloud that modern progress had necessitated the dispersal of such a famous stud of vanners. There was no doubt that she enjoyed herself, and that her keen companionship added greatly to her father's pleasure.

All too soon came the time when we had to leave these delights and keep our promise to meet her mother for tea.

" Oh, Daddy, but that was lovely," she said as we left. " I say, you and I are fools over horses, aren't we ?"

I agreed that we were, and suggested that anyone who was not a fool over something and somebody sometimes missed a lot of pleasure in life.

" Then we three don't miss much," came the reply. " I'm a fool over Mummy and you and horses ; Mummy's the same over you and me and p'raps clothes and poultry ; and you're one over Mummy and me and horses and all sorts of things."

" Here, steady on, young woman," I said. " What are the all sorts of things I'm a fool over ?"

" Oh ! Politics, and the countryside, and trespassers and golf, and bridge, and wasting time with friends, and arguing just for fun, and——"

" Here, that's enough," I cut in, thinking that the catalogue was far too long and too truthful, and that out of the mouths of young children comes sound truth. " Look ! There's Mummy and Vi."

" With their noses up against a window, Daddy," giggled my companion and critic. " Come on, I'm ravenous."

Tea over, we collected the spoils of the day, and drove back to the peace of Wilts without incident.

* * * * * *

Haymaking is nearly done, a modest cut and most of it only medium quality, for the thunderstorms have taken their toll. But by way of compensation they have made up the face of England most charmingly. Gone is the hard look of drought, and in its place the countryside smiles wherever you go. Everything looks so fresh and alive. The fields are a patchwork of green and gold and brown, and the gardens of England are altogether glorious, for roses are in bloom outside both cottage and castle.

Yesterday my wife and I went to the annual garden party at Royal Holloway College, and the beauty of the roses on the South Terrace was sumptuous. The sun shone, the turf was green, the roses were June's best blooms, and the girls' frocks—words fail me. No two were alike, yet all were lovely. If there is any prettier sight than hundreds of

English girls in flowery frocks enjoying themselves in such a perfect setting I have yet to witness it. In contrast, I must confess that the men present were the reverse of ornamental, but such was the glory of the day that even their drab attire failed to spoil yesterday's picture.

*   *   *   *   *   *

It rains and it rains and it rains, so much so that the fag end of haymaking in this district looks like being more trouble than the major part of it. Even so, my neighbours and I have been luckier than more western haymakers, for a conversation with a Somersetshire farmer to-day told me that down in the west country farmers had not carried any hay whatsoever.

" Most of it's gone in out of sight under the grass," he said, " and our land is so wet that we can't even hoe."

Any farmer in such a predicament has my deepest sympathy, for he is powerless to alter it. All he can do is to draw on his reserves of faith and patience, realize that " thur allus wur a time," and pray God that " thur zoon will be." But no matter how great his faith and patience, it is difficult for a farmer to keep cheerful this weather. Continuous rain day after day makes his surroundings look much more mournful and depressing at this time of year than at any other. The countryside is not garbed for such weather. It wears its heaviest clothing—green tweeds instead of mackintosh. Foliage drips, corn fields droop, the sun hides his face, the skies are leaden, and weeds flourish. In fact the only cheering thing to many farmers during the past week has been that the townsman has been compelled to suffer with them. The rain has washed out his sport along with the quality of their hay. Which sounds rather ungracious perhaps, but no one can say that it is not understandable.

*   *   *   *   *   *

To-day, in spite of hard storms nearly every hour, has been enlivened on this farm by a visit from the Cherub. Early in the spring he vanished from our ken into a racing stable, and we have missed his cheery smile and sound commonsense. Stable lad, budding jockey, or soon to be a trainer—call him what you will—the fact remains that he is still a little boy of engaging manners and the possessor of a sweet tooth. Just before the Derby he was buying some sweets in a village shop, and the shopkeeper inquired of him which horse was going to win the big race.

"If I knew, do you think I should be fool enough to waste my money on sweets?" came the reply.

But to-day he wasted his valuable time on us, and we were all very grateful, and better for it. Four feet something of country craft surveyed our foal in silence for several minutes, while Pam and I waited anxiously for the verdict.

"He's built all right, but at that age no one can tell how a colt's going to turn out. Sometimes their hocks go all to blazes by the time they're yearlings. But feed him, feed him well all next winter, and I'll come and have another look at him. He wants to be a full fifteen hands next year this time, and he won't be unless he gets plenty of grub."

Meekly we promised to obey orders, and in great trepidation we next presented Blackbird to the expert. He walked round this still rather gaunt animal again in silence, and I feared the worst. But no! Strange to say our latest purchase found favour.

"That ain't a bad horse at all," the Cherub said. "I

reckon he'll carry you well next season. Yes, I know he's a bit thin, but he's all right. I like that horse."

Gosh! What would I not give for such assurance? When people ask me about books I fairly dither at them, knowing full well that in reading matter one man's meat is another's poison all too often. But when it came to tea the Cherub was the same attractive little boy whom we had always known, and his new life does not seem to have spoiled him at all ; for which he has my great admiration. It takes a good colt to stand corn.

     *   *   *   *   *   *

Some friends came to tea to-day, and a rather curious conversation took place during the meal. There were six of us, three sets of parents, all about the same age, and all with children about the same age. One lady told us that one of her young hopefuls was about to sit for the School Certificate, and that she was worrying about his getting through. Apparently, for him to fail in this exam. would be considered a tragedy. Another mother agreed, and said that although her offspring was not taking this particular educational fence until next year, she was already worrying about their possible failure. So I suggested that there were other things in life besides the School Certificate.

" Does it matter so much if they don't pass it ?" I asked, a remark which was greeted with a chorus of protests that without this label any young of the human species was outside the pale of modern life.

" Well, I'm wondering whether that's as true as you seem to think. Look here, in a few years' time there'll be so many children who have passed the blame thing, that one who hasn't will be a rare article, and therefore will command a high price from employers. Why, they'll fight to get him, or possibly her."

This brought down a shower of condemnation on my head from everybody, my wife putting on the finishing touch by saying that I was hopeless, and that it was useless either to argue or listen to me.

" Give him some more strawberries," she said. "They'll perhaps keep him quiet,"

I refilled my plate with the fruit, waited until the icing sugar and cream had come my way, and then returned to the attack.

" Look here," I said to my neighbour at the table. " Have you passed the School Certificate ?"

" No ! " she said. " You see, I never had the chance."

" Quite, but you're still alive," I chuckled. " Now then, let's take a census round the table."

This we did, to find that no one present had passed the School Certificate or any other official examination. Whereupon I proceeded to swank on our behalf most blatantly.

" There you are," I said in triumph, " not one of us. We're all uneducated, and yet we've all earned our livings, paid our debts, and our taxes, kept out of gaol, got married, raised a family, and avoided divorce. Where in England, or in the whole world for that matter, could you find six people round one table who have such a record ? Dash it ! The nation ought to put us in charge of the Board of Education, pay us fabulous salaries, and erect statues to us when we pass out."

" With an inscription ' They never passed the School Certificate,' I suppose ?" chuckled one man. " I say, you're an awful ass, but I'm more than half on your side over this."

And, although I agree with him that I am an awful ass concerning this and many other matters, as long as a sufficient proportion of English fathers are more than half on my side in the necessary ridiculing of the fearsome respect which most mothers pay to the School Certificate, there may be a hope for the next few generations of English children.

* * * * * *

Still it rains, and, as a result, my trimmings are fast disappearing underneath the grass. Still, we have managed to tuck and top and thatch all the hayricks which we have made save one. And that one is too hot to have its hat on. Curiously enough it is the first rick we put up, and it was made in two goes. I knew full well that the first chunk of it was hardly fit to stack, and when the weather permitted us to have the second go, I took the precaution to pull the middle out and fit up an air-hole with hurdles right through its middle.

That was done nearly a month ago, but from the sour smell which has prevaded my car every time I have driven up the lane I have known that this rick was plenty hot enough. However, having never yet managed to burn a rick by internal combustion—a grave reflection on my farming capabilities, for it implies that I have never carried my hay " gay " enough—I have steadfastly refused to make a close examination of this rick, notwithstanding the pleadings and dire prophecies of Jim the drowner. But when farming errors become too glaring one's neighbours call one to account.

This morning, being cross with the weather and crosser still because I was behind schedule with some writing, I left word that I was not to be disturbed unless it was for something very important ; and then retired to a back bedroom which had been turned into a workroom and refuge from callers. I had just got nicely going, when a message came that Mr. So-and-so had called to see me. Now this man was a friend, and as friendship should ever come before work, I went down to see him.

After greetings and lamentations concerning the weather he came to the reason for his call.

" Of course, I know I stand the chance of being told to mind my own business," he said, " but you've got a rick up the road that's too hot to be safe."

" Rubbish," I said. " There's a hole right through the middle of him. He's all right even if he is a bit warm." Why a rick is always a " he " in farming conversation I know not, but such is the case.

" H'm, ye-e-s ! He's got a hole in him, 'tis true, but he's dangerously hot at either end. He smelt so sour that I stopped my car, and put my iron into him. He's a hundred and eighty degrees one end, and a hundred and seventy the other."

" And what's firin' point ? " I asked.

" Two hundred or thereabouts. Look here, he's worse than you think. Come up and have a look with me. My car's outside."

Now why one's friends should bother with one's mistakes beats me, but they do ; and so I meekly went up the lane with him. And that rick was hot, devilish hot ; so hot that I promised to deal with it immediately after lunch, a meal which I wanted my friend to share. But he had another appointment for which he was already late, and I could not even coax him to have a drink. All he was worried about was whether he had offended me by his interference. God bless him ! I thanked him for his kindness, and told him that I did not think it was possible that he could ever offend me.

" Bless you, Bill," I said. " You're a Good Samaritan !

He chuckled as he started his car, and said, " Well, this morning I didn' pass by on the other side, did I ? "

As a result we have been attending to that rick this afternoon. By golly ! It was hot, all right. We cut a hole in each end with a hay knife, each large enough to work in and each about seven feet deep. And a lot of the stuff we threw out was almost black. But we have let the heat out, and next week we shall be able to top up and thatch that rick quite safely.

Usually when a farmer has a rick which gets so hot as to need this " cutting out " treatment, his men trot out the old saying, " 'tis cheaper to spoil it in field than in rick," but this so-called haytime has been so wet that my stalwarts all agree that this rick of hay is much better where it is, in spite of the loss by the overheating of a certain portion.

But how the smell of over-heated hay clings to one's clothing ! When we had finished that job, it announced our presence to anyone within a hundred yards down wind.

* * * * * *

On grass land which has been well stocked, copious rains at this time of year always spoil hay and bring some mushrooms. Such is the position of a farmer whose farm abuts on to a town that it is with great difficulty that I manage to obtain enough mushrooms for the family breakfast, although my farm is providing numerous other folk with mushrooms ad lib. One growls in private when these folk pick one's mushrooms in order to eat them ; but when they pick them and sell them, as many of my neighbours have been doing recently, one becomes annoyed, and I think justifiably.

But in either case one is powerless to stop the nuisance. As I mentioned before in this notebook, townspeople expect to get something for nothing from the countryside, and their voting strength is such that usually they get it. The best way of meeting their selfish habits is for the farmer to " forgive them, for they know not what they do " ; and just now to hope for some fine weather.

* * * * * *

As usual this wet haytime has brought forth a crop of suggestions in the papers that the British farmer deserves to have his hay spoilt, because he does not haymake on the lines of the Highland farmer, and deal with his hay by some variant of the tripod system.

That this method does enable fair quality hay to be saved during wet weather I am well aware, but I should doubt whether South-country farmers would be better off by adopting it. It is foolish to criticize any farming method in the light of one year's weather ; and my experience has been that nine years out of ten the prevailing method of haymaking in this district is the cheapest and most efficient possible. In a season such as this one gets caught, perhaps, but the average for ten years is always a good one.

But I must confess that I should like to see the sun again.

* * * * * *

This Summer of our Discontent

I felt that it was useless to continue with a chapter entitled " Haytime," because instead it is mud time. In fact, it seems waste of time to try to make hay, or rather to try to dry the muck which now occupies many hayfields sufficiently to put it into a rick. Three times have I tried to scratch up some trimmings, and three times the rain has come before it was half dry.

Yesterday morning we turned a field of muck, and at four o'clock it was still too wet to rick, so I went for a drive in the evening, just to get away from the sight of it. Passing by a neighbour's fields I saw his men and motor cars busily ricking some woefully discoloured hay, at which sight I felt very aggrieved. " How the dickens can he carry hay, when I can't ? " I muttered.

This evening, after a showery day, he called to see me, and I told him of my grievance.

" You needn't have worried," he said. " 'Twer muck. I never went to look at it. I told my fellows to begin after tea, and when I drove down to the gate of the field the rickmaker called out, ' Yer, hast thee 'ad a look at this ? ' ' No ! ' I shouted. ' And I ain't goin' to. I don't care whether 'tis hay, dung, or silage—you put it into a heap so that I shan't see it layin' about to-morrow morning.' Fact o' it, I valued the aftergrass more'n the hay."

*   *   *   *   *   *

Being a trifle work-worn, I feel constrained to write about work. It is a thing of which I have had some intimate knowledge during the past few days—I have not only seen it done, but I, myself, have done a little. Goodness knows, I have every reason to be grateful for more than my share of good fortune, which enables me to lead an interesting and exciting life, and to keep the wolf from the door ; but I am fast realizing that life was much simpler and less tiring when my activities were confined to farming and milk retailing—and I defy anyone to say that either of those callings is suited to a lazy temperament such as mine. Three days in town on business last week, one day up there this week, add on some writing against time, throw into the mixture come caddling haymaking weather, and the result has been, as I say, rather exhausting.

I'm sick and tired of vainly trying to get my trimmings dry enough to rick. In fact I know nothing which gets my goat like haymaking. Farmer friends say to me, " All very well for you. You don't need to worry about it. You can just hire some men, and sit down happily to work at your desk, knowing that if the weather's good your chaps will make good hay, that if it's bad they'll do just as well without you and probably better, and that anyway you're on a good wicket."

It sounds marvellous, and I will admit that in bad weather my staff does very much better without my gloomy face in the field ; but I defy any farmer to write very happily even when his hay is being well made for him by willing workers such as mine. It's silly, and perhaps childish, but there's no doubt that the hay comes first in one's mind. And when the weather won't permit haymaking, one's scribbling suffers still more.

To-morrow morning I am going to the Royal Show at Bristol ; but, as usual, now that I am not wholly a farmer, the pleasure of the day is to be marred with the awful thought that I have to write and deliver some two thousand words about the Show by six p.m. A writer's work like a woman's is never done. Even when he is apparently amusing himself his mind must be ever storing up material which may someday come in useful.

I am rather worried about to-morrow's job, for I have no experience of this quick journalism. Also I am very conscious that I possess the traditionally slow mind of the countryman. When I do find a subject I prefer to let it mature in my mind for at least a week ; to think about it whilst I am driving a car or riding round the countryside ; and then, when it is ripe, to set about its harvesting. But to-morrow I shall be compelled to gather the seed before tea, and produce the crop in a bare two hours. Ugh ! Yet another instance of the modern craze for speed.

*   *   *   *   *   *

Gosh, I'm tired this morning ! I did my job at the Royal yesterday, but it has taken it out of me. Any man who tries to see everything at the Royal in one day is attempting the impossible ; and, although I worked hard yesterday, the show was too big for me, and I never saw half of it.

But no agricultural show can be too big, for to be big is one of its chief functions. Although ostensibly its object is to provide an opportunity for manufacturers to show their newest goods to possible customers, and for farmers to exhibit their stock in competition with their fellows, its most important job is to illustrate to townsfolk the size and importance of our farming industry. I have long held the view that the average townsman or townswoman can comprehend only what he or she can see ; and that, because farming possesses nothing large or spectacular like the Queen Mary, it is difficult, save in times of famine, to focus public opinion upon it. But yesterday's visit to the Royal has made me change my mind. The Royal is definitely much bigger than the Queen Mary, just as our farming industry is so much bigger and more important than our shipbuilding. So, in connection with this point the Royal can pat itself on the back—that is, of course, if an agricultural show has a back to pat.

After entering it yesterday I soon felt like Gulliver in Brobdingnag, and any townsman after strolling through it for half an hour must have felt constrained to misquote the Queen of Sheba, and say, " They never told me the half of farming's activities and greatness." Indeed, the farther he explored the more amazed he must have been at the manifold trades and professions which do business with modern farming—engineering, rubber, electricity, chemistry, veterinary science, biology, education, insurance, broadcasting, the manufacture of feeding stuffs and other necessaries from commodities produced in every country in the world. The catalogue seemed endless.

As a spectacle to impress and entertain the town visitor the show could not be criticized, but as an attempt to educate him concerning farming I could not help wondering whether the arrangement of the exhibits was the best possible. I walked seemingly endless miles through buzzing machinery and inventions of all kinds. Like the Irishman, I would sooner walk ten miles than stand five, but in the interests of farming I stood for at least twenty miles talking to this trader and that expert, and poking my nose into all sorts of weird contraptions.

I offended one gentleman, I'm afraid, for when he asked me if I was interested in one prodigious contrivance I told him I was more interested in the mentality of the man who wished to let loose such a Brontosaurus in God's Green England. His retort was that progress was everything. Whereupon I countered that progress which robbed civilized life of grace, instead of adding that precious quality, was not progress at all. In this I was supported by another farmer, who, on overhearing our conversation, said, "Guv'nor, you're quite right. I met one of those things on the road late the other night and I was so frightened that I damn near passed out."

So I passed on through more progress. I saw sterilizers, medicines, feeding stuffs from Africa and Egypt, and implements from our old enemy Germany (not the worst shown by any means). I wandered through serried ranks of rubber-tyred vehicles. I inspected haymaking and harvesting machines galore. I was educated at the Ministry of Agriculture's tent, and instructed in the way I should go by the National Mark people ; and I saw so much of science and invention and education that before long I was not only bewildered but tired.

" This is no good," I said to myself. " After all, this is supposed to be an agricultural show. But where the dickens is the agriculture ? I'm a farmer not a townsman. I haven't come to be amused with a Meccano set or thrilled by the sight of horses jumping. I'm here on business. I'm sick of the stink of petrol. I prefer the scent of dung. Where are the natural things which make all this buzzing clattering work of man's hands possible ? Where are the things in farming which pay the rent, buy all the implements, grow all the crops, and pay all the tithes and manifold other

bills of this great industry ?   In other words, where is (or
should it be where are ?) the livestock.

I looked around.   There were, it is true, a few horses
to be seen in the large show ring, but, after all, work horses
are power, and light horses are play.   I glanced at the clock.
The time was nearly one.   Lunch was indicated ;   but,
again in the interests of farming, I continued at work.   I
refused to look at the Farmers' Club pavilion, with its chairs
and its white-aproned waitresses.   I passed by on the other
side ;   deliberately forgetting that my flesh was weak, that
breakfast was almost six hours away, that beer was best,
and Guinness good for me. I refused the proffered hospitality
of friends.   I ignored the National Farmers' Union, and
risked the fact that I had not insured with them against
every eventuality.   Onward ever onward I stepped out
upon my aching feet, in search of the things which made the
show possible, and which constitute some three-quarters of
British agriculture—cattle, sheep, pigs and poultry.
Neither food nor drink should pass my lips, I decided, until
I had found the really important branch of farming.

Let me be quite fair to the Royal.   I found the livestock
all right, and so did every other person in the show who was
interested in them.   But I question whether the average
town visitor did find them, and this, I think, was a pity.
Any agricultural show—and especially the Royal—is
agriculture's showroom.   In it our great farming industry
places its best and most important goods.   At such a show
British agriculture tells the world of its greatness ; and yet
the really important thing in our farming—the inward
monetary grace—was shoved away into the back window
of the showroom ;   what time the outward and visible
sign was given the front one.

No doubt the answer to this criticism will be, as Mrs. Beeton said, " First catch your hare," and that, unless farming's " Meccano set " was put near the entrance of the show, the townsman would not visit it. But apart from this I have nothing but praise for the arrangements.

And now to get to business—or rather to the livestock. In this department the British farmer can challenge the world without much fear, and it is round the judging rings that one finds the real Royal Agricultural Show. Here one sees the pundits of each particular breed and class of livestock, and while the stock is judged by the judges, the judges are judged by the onlookers. Indeed, it is no exaggeration to say that the stock is not judged anything like so harshly as its judges.

But no one attains the honour of being a judge at the Royal without having the necessary qualifications and the guts to do the job properly ; and, while of necessity some exhibitors must be disappointed, I have never yet heard any serious criticism of the awards. For the Royal judges have the courage of their convictions, and make no attempt to achieve the impossible by pleasing everybody. Consequently, they please everybody, being like Caesar's wife, above suspicion.

But it is in the judging rings that one can obtain an insight into the human side of the show. What hopes are dashed and what little personal tragedies take place ! That pig or heifer or ram lamb may be the year's work of some herdsman. True, his master may have found the money, but in many—aye, in most—cases it is the employee who has given of himself in order that his charges shall earn fame at the Royal. Imperturbably the men and their charges parade in line ahead. Silently they obey the judge's orders. But when a beast is moved from first place to second, can anyone blame the herdsman if his face falls ?

Having spent an hour with the cattle I ate a much-needed lunch, and then went to have a look at the pigs and sheep. Nice things pigs. They lay in their pens—obese, supine, and peaceful. What fortunate animals ! No rush, no worry, nothing to sell, no article to write—they just let the Royal world go by, unheeding. Porcine snores filled every pen, reminding me of the sittingroom of a Victorian household on a Sunday afternoon.

But when the judging began ! What hectic activity ! I thought of the old nursery rhyme, " Tom, Tom, the piper's son, stole a pig, and away he run." That sort of thing would have been out of court at the Royal yesterday. There it was Tom's son who owned a pig, and he didn't run. On the contrary he ambled, and so did his pig. One man, one pig, one wooden batten to steer him or her, and gently does it, was the motto. Huge pigs, medium pigs, and little pigs. All went the same way into the ring, and all returned to their pens by the same route ; some with rosettes and some without, but all with bacon in the offing.

After an hour of this I decided that too much pig society would make the morrow's rasher lose its charm, so I departed to the sheep. Here I found a different atmosphere. The judges and the spectators were the same, but the sheep were so much more modern in their appearance than either cattle or pigs. Coquettes they were. Made up, yea verily, like the most modern of young ladies ; or, as one scornful critic put it to me, " Like a bloomin' dog's dinner." In varying shades of yellow and amber they made sheep's eyes at their judge and jury. Someday, I thought, their life will end in mint sauce, but at the Royal it is a flaunt in their best clothes, and sufficient for the day is the glory thereof.

But, as I don't keep any sheep, their flirting held no message for me, so I decided to visit the poultry in order to gain some information concerning my latest farming love—geese. Unfortunately, I discovered that the poultry tent was not due to open until next day. I must admit that I have no grouse about this, for it was stated in the catalogue and, I presume, advertised in the Press. However, not being aware of this, I suppose I was the only goose on exhibition yesterday.

From there I ambled round the show again. More livestock, more implements, more education, and more—a lot more—friendship. At the Royal one meets everybody —farmers whom you have not seen for twenty years ; old schoolfellows ; critics who try to make you stand up to what you wrote some years ago ; friends who tell you that you are talking out of the back of your neck ; and one-time farm pupils who suffered your dominion in their green youth. Oh, I found that the Royal was a great educator.

At four o'clock I sat down in the Farmers' Club pavilion to write out my impressions, and at first I could not get going. Never before had I tried to write with the conversation of some fifty or sixty people in my ears. For the first quarter of an hour I could not write a line, but before I could panick over this the varied languages and dialects around me provided the key which unlocked my muddled mind, and enabled me to finish the job to time. German, French, Canadian, Australian, and American speech opposed each other in varying twangs, telling me that other countries still have something to learn from the British farmer. Mingled with these, the soft U of Devon, the slurred Z of Wilts, humorous Lancashire, broad Yorkshire, unintelligible

Welsh, and the talk of Caledonia's stern and wild farmers, all told me that the Royal was the right place for overseas farmers to acquire the knowledge they seek. Indeed, perhaps the last mentioned is the greatest compliment which I can pay to the Royal Agricultural Society of England—even the canny Scot considers it worth his while to travel right down to Bristol to visit its annual show !

But to me the chief impression of this year's Royal was one of size. There seemed to be no end to it, and the setting was ideal. From the moment I entered the gates the rest of England seemed to be very far away. Bristol had vanished ; the ubiquitous council house was not ; my car seemed lost for ever ; and in a vast showroom surrounded by tall trees and roofed with an English sky, I wandered through and wondered at the manifold marvels of British farming.

And to-day, as a result, I'm dog-tired, and it's still raining.

*   *   *   *   *   *

A wet night and a drizzle all morning having put paid to any haymaking for to-day, this afternoon I escorted Pam to a local gymkhana. The weather managed to hold up for a few hours, we met a lot of friends, and we had a thoroughly good time. But the fly in the ointment was the behaviour of Master Thomas Webster.

He put up a very poor show in the bending race, but we had great hopes of the novice jumping. We watched the open jumping with interest and admiration ; and, when this was finished and a lower set of jumps put up, we got ready for the struggle. Tom is so lazy on grass that I told Pam to try him over a hurdle outside the ring, just to show him that he was there on business bent. He cleared this in fine style, and a few moments afterwards was in the ring, ready to do or die. At least, his rider was in that state of mind, but Thomas had other views as to the best way of spending a summer afternoon.

Twice he stuck his toes in at the brush jump, but at the third attempt he came over to the manner born. After this I had great hopes of him completing the course, but he let us down badly. Two little white rails—I swear not more than two feet high—he refused ignominiously, and great was his rider's disappointment. I comforted her by telling her that it was my fault, in that up to date I had not found time to put up some white show jumps for her to practise over. So we came away, full of plans which will enable us to fight successfully another day. As I write I can see Master Tom gutting steadily in the pasture outside. He little knows what trials lie in store.

*　　*　　*　　*　　*　　*

Yesterday was taken up with another visit to the Royal Show, this time in order to carry out a broadcasting job ; and, as usual, it rained little or much all day. I arrived to time at noon, and by eight p.m. there was no more tired body of toilers in the Royal than the B.B.C. officials and engineers from the Western Regional, together with some half-dozen broadcasters including myself, who sploshed from point to point in an endeavour to build up what is technically known as an Outside Broadcast. What some of us called it long before it actually took place is definitely not printable—rain being just as bad for Outside Broadcasts as it is for hay and shows.

My job was to talk for a few minutes about the livestock, someone else dealt with the machinery, another with buttermaking, the whole thing being wound by the

Buggins family, to whose creator, Miss Mabel Constanduros goes the palm of this particular O.B. Her especial brand of humour always possesses a sufficiency of that necessary quality, truth ; which invariably makes it not only more entertaining but so much more valuable.

Granny Buggins was a scream, granted ; but when she wanted to " rouse up " the rural population, on the lines that it would " do 'em good," many farming listeners even must have agreed with her. When she wanted the show animals to do some tricks—what a delicate jibe at the ignorance of so many townsfolk ! And her desire to prove that the bull wasn't padded ! Granny, there was no flies on you !

But at eight p.m., when broadcasters had ceased from troubling and were wearily seeking rest, there were a dickens of a lot of folk still at work in the show yard. For aught I know many of them were busy all night, for it takes all sorts of people busy during all sorts of hours to make a " Royal " show. To the average visitor a show is a day out, even when he or she—and what a lot of shes are interested in farming matters nowadays—does some business there. But there must be hundreds of workers at the show— waiters, stockmen and stockmaidens, car park attendants, those responsible for water supplies, sanitation, and making the roads passable in wet weather, and officials of every kind—all hard at work, and all, I should imagine, tired and thankful when the week was over.

*   *   *   *   *   *

Tom Webster's education progressed a long way this evening. A neighbour rang up to tell Pam that she had erected a course of jumps exactly similar to the one's at the gymkhana the other day, and would she like to bring Tommy over and try them ?   Hastily the ever-gutting Tom was removed from his pasture, and a few minutes later he was carrying his mistress to his school.

Neither her mother nor I was able to be present in class, but later in the evening we were regaled with the story of Master Tom's behaviour by a flushed and excited little girl who should have been asleep two hours before.

" Oh, Daddy !   He was awful.   He jumped the hurdle, and the brush, and the in and out, but he just funked the triple bar, even when we took off the top rail.   However, we made him jump it after a bit, and then he sailed over the full triple like a bird."

" Well, that's all right.   What else did you have a go at ? "

" An imitation wall, Daddy, made of wood painted red. I don't know what Miss Blank must be saying about Tom. He just knelt on her wall, and abolished it.   And we had to get a hammer and nails and remake it."

" And then ? "

" Oh, the next time he jumped about four times too high, but after that he went over it fine, several times.   And Miss Blank says that I can go over any evening just to keep him in training.   Isn't that gorgeous ? "

Both her mother and I agreed that it was gorgeous, and wished her good night ;   but I doubt whether either of us was telling the truth.   Still, it would be worse than silly to put any suspicion of fear into Pam's mind.   She is entirely concerned with her pony's performance, and never once considers her own, which is far better than she knows.   No matter whether Tom jumps well or awkwardly, refuses flatly or, even kneels on walls, Pam is still in the saddle when he has finished. I just hate to think where her father would arrive after similar trials.

While motoring from Shaftesbury to Salisbury the other day a friend and I had occasion to remark on several cases of dangerous driving, and my companion summed up this far too prevalent nuisance by saying, " You know, competition between drivers causes far more accidents than speed."

Always I have believed competition to be a good thing, but I must admit that his remark has shaken that faith badly. It is so very true. In their eagerness to steal a march on the other fellow numerous car drivers do things which should result in them being sentenced to twelve months' hard without option. Does competition in all phases of civilized life bring about similar troubles ? I do not know, but I have decided in the future to overhaul very carefully every form of competition before I give it my unqualified blessing.

The more I think about the many instances of selfish and dangerous driving which one sees on the roads to-day the more convinced I am that our speed cops on fast motor cycles should be replaced by stationary cops, who should be dressed in mufti and seated at their ease in deck chairs at suitable spots along the roads. Any man so placed over-looking a long and very gradual bend would be certain to see at least a hundred cases of dangerous driving every week.

But, even if competition and bad manners generally be two of the chief causes of motor accidents, there is no gainsaying that the increased speed of road traffic is still the major cause. I am not surprised at the number of people who are killed and injured every week ; rather am I amazed that the number of casualties is not ten times as great. To my mind, considering the average skill and manners of road users to-day, the small number of accidents is a great advertisement of the efficiency and safety of modern motor vehicles. Even so, to permit their present speed on our existing roads is criminal. On a road restricted solely for motor traffic such speed and much greater speed would be permissible; but on a public highway, which is used by old and infirm people, young children, and animals, it is wicked.

Ardent motorists can yap till doomsday to the effect that speed is not dangerous. They forget the really important point—that while we have about doubled the speed of road traffic during the last thirty years, the speed at which the human being can jump out of the way of it has remained unchanged. It is still the speed of Adam—probably less, for I have a notion that our ancestor, in spite of his severely punished weakness for apples, was a more athletic person than the average pedestrian of the twentieth century.

*   *   *   *   *   *

What a lot of hay has been spoilt in the field, and what a lot of grass has been spoilt by being left standing ! Driving by a field of the latter the other evening—needless to say it was raining—I remarked to my companion that by the time the weather permitted that field to be mown the crop would be valueless.

He gazed over the hedge and snorted. " Brown as an old hat, not much better'n straw," was his comment. " That'll want to be put in rick the day before 'tis cut."

Which was a countryman's way of saying that the grass was weeks too old. But in such a summer as this, what can the owner of it do but watch it spoil ?

This morning my postbag contained some verses which seemed very applicable to the farmer's fate this season.

I am taking the liberty of quoting them in full, without even the customary acknowledgment, as my correspondent wrote that she did not know the name of their author.

> A farmer knocked at the pearly gate,
> His face was scarred and old ;
> He stood before the Man of Fate
> For admission to the fold.
>
> " What have you done," St. Peter asked,
> " To gain admission here ? "
> " I've been a farmer, Sir," he said,
> " For many and many a year."
>
> The pearly gate swung open wide,
> As St. Peter touched the bell ;
> " Come in," he said, " and choose your harp,
> You've had your taste of hell ! "

This year the farmer's particular hell has been a very wet one.

* * * * * *

In spite of the wet the corn harvest draws near, for already the winter oats are turning colour, and one or two pieces in the district are already up in aisle. This evening, whilst hunting for a reference, I turned up a cutting from the *Implement and Machinery Review*, dated August, 1904, which someone had sent me some time ago. Its title was " Harvesting by steam in Wiltshire," and an illustration showed a six h.p. Foden compound traction engine pulling a seven foot Albion binder through a crop of oats near Alton Priors, on the farm of a Mr. James Stratton.

From that, I thought, to last week's show of mechanical

harvesting tackle at the Royal. All down the ages the British farmer has pressed the latest invention into the land's service as soon as it became at all practicable so to do. And this thought led to another—that it is high time that there was more truth and less eyewash talked about finding employment for much greater numbers of our people on the agricultural land of this country.

In every branch of farming science and invention are displacing man-power, and more and more in the near future will these influences displace man-power. Consequently, it would seem that all those who advocate wholesale land settlement, no matter what the cost and without an agricultural policy which calls for greater increased production from our land, are either unthinking fools or conscious liars. Even with a policy which insisted on intensive production from every acre of our remaining agricultural land—when one takes into consideration the future reduction of our farming acreage by town encroachment, together with the effect on agricultural employment of the future discoveries of our scientists and inventors—it is absurd to blind oneself to the probability that ten years hence there will be fewer people working in agriculture on this island, and ten years later fewer still. We all know this, and to my mind it is wicked not to discuss it in the open.

* * * * * *

This year I have endeavoured to keep an eye on the effect of rain on St. Swithin's Day, which is supposed to presage rain every day for forty days afterwards. Up to date the old prophecy has proved correct. If it doesn't rain in the morning, it rains in the afternoon. If it doesn't rain in the afternoon, it rains in the morning, or the rain comes on after tea just when many people have managed to get some spoiled hay dry enough to rick. And when it doesn't rain either in the morning, the afternoon, or the evening, it rains all day, just to show us what July can do when it is properly upset.

To-day it has performed the last-mentioned feat, continuous rain from dawn till dusk—a day when farm work was impossible, obviously for me a day for writing. But a fruitless hour at my desk confirmed something which has been worrying me greatly during the past few weeks—that if a wet summer is bad for haymaking and farming generally, it is the reverse of helpful to anyone whose business it is to write about country life. There is, has been for some time, and apparently will be in the immediate future nothing to write about save rain, and it would take a much cleverer man than I to make that subject interesting to anyone.

So I was overjoyed when a disgruntled farmer friend turned up to spend the day. Having done our best to dry up the wet with the high temperature of our language, we switched over to politics in order to cool off. My companion was definitely left wing in his ideas, and I pleaded guilty to his accusation that I was neither one thing nor another, neither fascist nor socialist, but a two-faced muddled thinker.

" You're a representative of what somebody, Wyndham Lewis, I think, calls the soft centre of the population," he triumphed. " No blooming good to anybody, not even to yourself."

To which I countered with, " But, my lad, remember that it's the ham in the social sandwich that really matters."

" Whose porcine point of view is illustrated weekly in Punch," he sneered. From which point we both forgot the rain, and got down to business.

I tried to tell him that the fact that in one issue Punch could pull the legs of such widely different folk as Mr. Lloyd George, Mr. Stanley Baldwin, Hitler, Mussolini, ardent fascists and equally ardent socialists, the surrealist school of art, the town trespasser, and the irate farmer, proved the superiority of the English over every other nation. " In any other country," I suggested, " the people responsible for such leg-pulling would be gaoled, hung, or worse."

He growled something to the effect that in this country it was high time that people who joked about politics were subjected to some form of discipline.

" Damn it ! " he said. " Politics do matter. Look what you can do to better people's conditions through the medium of politics."

I demanded an illustration, and he chose the subject of electric light.

" Everybody should be compelled to use it," he argued. " Then, we should all get it for about no pence a unit. You cannot deny that the result of such discipline would confer a great boon."

" H'm, materially, I grant, but against that we should have lost a much more important thing, the right of choice. Look here, there are many things in your past life which you regret, but there have been some things in it which you wouldn't have missed for anything ? "

He nodded assent.

" Well, just make a list of 'em in your mind, and I'll bet you that not one of 'em's anything material like electric light."

" True," he admitted, " but that isn't the point——"

" It is the point. An Englishman can enjoy life without electric light, but he can't enjoy it without the liberty to poke fun at the leaders of the nation, royal, political, industrial, or artistic."

" But if people are on the poverty line, haven't got the necessary wherewithal to live decently, they must have material benefits before they can enjoy the daft things you set such store by."

" Possibly yes, and possibly no. I reckon that there are thousands of poor people in this country to-day, who would prefer to have their existing standard of living and our Royal Family, than a doubled income coupled with the disappearance of our Royal Family. Hundreds of women, charwomen if you like, would prefer to read about Princess Marina's baby by candlelight, than about a socialist dictator's baby by electric light. Why, many of them get as much kick out of the former as they would in having a baby of their own. Illogical, silly, a thing which you may consider so degrading that it should be altered, by force if necessary, but for all that very human and very true."

" But," he snorted, " So—I'll use your own word—so degrading that any form of compulsion to alter it would be justified. Such people need saving from themselves."

" In your eyes, but not in theirs. You consider any clever political plan which would confer a material benefit upon people to be more important than the people themselves. Anyone who would not conform or who hindered the plan you would remove by force, just like all dictators. You want to put everybody into an expensive material strait jacket provided by the State ; most folk would prefer a shabby waistcoat of their own design."

And so we wrangled quite amicably until he left, sometimes one making a point and sometimes the other. After he had gone I thought over the argument, and was bound to admit that in many things he undoubtedly had the better of me, but that in the matter of the great value to mankind of non-material things I was supporting something very sound.

*   *   *   *   *   *

This morning came a frantic call for the MS. of this notebook, so I have spent the day in reading it through, with the result that I am almost afraid to let it go to the printers in its present form.   It is such a frightful give-away. Again and again it illustrates the correctness of the criticisms of my friend of yesterday—that I am a muddled thinker, two-faced, and precious little good to anybody ; and that I do not know how to sort or value the harvest of my year's moonraking.

Yet there does seem to be one thing which rings true throughout—a plea for a more general realization that there are a few important things in life in addition to man's cleverness. The beauty of a summer's sky, the goodness of a fine May morning, the wholesomeness of rural space and privacy, the healing comfort of natural quiet, the gift of love, the joy of children, the priceless boon of friendship, the knowledge that the innate goodness in man greatly outweighs the evil, and the loveliness of England's fair countryside at all seasons of the year. Little things, simple things, and natural things, but all precious things ; the value of which, through our cleverness, we are in some danger of forgetting.

Muddled or not, I see no reason to be ashamed of such a plea, and as I look out of the window I am convinced that it is a right one.   I want to begin cutting my wheat.   I have the crop, the men, and the implements, and yet I cannot start my corn harvest.   No State System, no clever plan, and no dictator can help me. And yet I do not worry. Why ? Because my muddled moonraking life has given me the faith to wait in patience for God's good time.

And I shall be very grateful indeed when He permits the sun to shine again on His to-day's so very green England.

* * * * * *

OXFORD

MORE OXFORD PAPERBACKS

Details of a selection of other books follow. A complete list of Oxford Paperbacks, including The World's Classics, Twentieth-Century Classics, OPUS, Past Masters, Oxford Authors, Oxford Shakespeare, and Oxford Paperback Reference, is available in the UK from the General Publicity Department, Oxford University Press (JN), Walton Street, Oxford OX2 6DP.

In the USA, complete lists are available from the Paperbacks Marketing Manager, Oxford University Press, 200 Madison Avenue, New York, NY 10016.

Oxford Paperbacks are available from all good bookshops. In case of difficulty, customers in the UK can order direct from Oxford University Press Bookshop, 116 High Street, Oxford, Freepost, OX1 4BR, enclosing full payment. Please add 10 per cent of published price for postage and packing.

FARMER'S GLORY

A. G. Street

First published in 1932, *Farmer's Glory* is a portrait of farming
life in southern England and eastern Canada in the first quarter
of the century. In his book, A. G. Street recalls the farming
practices and traditions of the pre-war years with affection
and respect, and the many changes in agricultural methods
that took place during the 1920s with great sorrow. *Farmer's
Glory* is a unique record of the pace and mode of life that has
now all but vanished.

THE WESTERN ISLAND

Robin Flower

Dr. Flower spent a considerable amount of time between 1910
and 1930 living amongst the 150 inhabitants of the Great
Blasket Island. He tells of the adversities and frugality of the
Gaelic-speaking people, of the folk-tales and the stories of
ghosts and fairies and poets.

STILL GLIDES THE STREAM

Flora Thompson

Like her well-loved trilogy *Lark Rise to Candleford,* this book depicts the vanished life of the countryside which Flora Thompson knew as a child in the 1880s. Cast in a fictional form, it is an enchanting portrait of an Oxfordshire village and its inhabitants around the time of Queen Victoria's Golden Jubliee.

'reading it is a perfect pleasure' Benny Green

OUR VILLAGE

Mary Russell Mitford

The little village of Three Mile Cross in Berkshire was Mary Russell Mitford's home for thirty years. She has drawn on her observations of the locality for many of her short essays, the best of which appear in this book, to give a unique picture of country life in the early years of the nineteenth century. Village events and festivals are described in vivid detail, as are the many colourful characters who peopled the small neighbour-hood.

COUNTRYMAN ON THE MOORS

John C. Atkinson

John Atkinson arrived in the remote parish of Danby in North Yorkshire in 1850 and was to remain on the moors until his death fifty years later. A keen archaeologist and local historian, he found particular pleasure in recounting the ancient folklore of the Dales with its unique superstitions and customs. His writing is often humorous, but also sensitive, and shows a deep love of the wild country he made his home.

A YEOMAN FARMER'S SON

A Leicestershire Childhood

H. St G. Cramp

The author describes his childhood in the village of Tur Langton in Leicestershire in the 1920s. 'A marvellous account of a family, a farm, and a village, written with verve and gusto.' *Dorset Life*

THE JOURNAL OF A COUNTRY PARISH

Robin Page

From his Cambridgeshire farm the author shows us the realities of life in his village and the surrounding fields through one year. 'Robin Page has captured all the flavour and charm of his own countryside.' Gordon Beningfield.

LIFTING THE LATCH

A Life on the Land

Sheila Stewart

For nearly eighty years Mont Abbot has lived and worked on the land near Enstone in Oxfordshire. This extraordinary record of his life and times was constructed by Sheila Stewart from a series of taped conversations.

THE DIARY OF A COUNTRY PARSON,
1758–1802

James Woodforde

Edited by John Beresford

James Woodforde was parson at Weston Longeville, Norfolk, from 1774 till his death in 1803. His life was obscure and tranquil, his character uncomplicated; he loved his country, sport, good food, and established institutions, and was warm-hearted and generous. His diary covers nearly every single day in his life from 1758 to 1802. What makes it a classic as well as a remarkable document of social history is Parson Woodforde's rare ability to bring vividly to life the rural England of two centuries ago.

'compulsive reading' *The Times*

Oxford Letters & Memoirs

ON THE PIG'S BACK

Bill Naughton

'After the appearance of *A Roof Over Your Head* Bill Naughton's writing was said to have "a quality of genius", an assessment amply borne out by this memoir.' *Times Educational Supplement*

The genius tribute came from a review by John Betjeman. Such acclaim for his work indicated that Bill Naughton's ambition to write had been amply fulfilled. But how a one-time coal-heaver and lorry driver turned to writing in the first place makes an absorbing narrative—with exceptional advice to anyone inclined to the literary life.

Bill Naughton's 'autobiographical excursion' takes him (and us) back through war-time London to County Mayo, his birth-place, and to pre-war Bolton, scene of his later boyhood. It is both a story and a social document, full of fresh detail.

'Reading this wise, tender, perceptive book is like being there—and no writer can hope to achieve more than that.' *London Evening Standard*

THE DILLEN

Angela Hewins

George Hewins was born in a Stratford doss-house at the zenith of the Victorian age. Barely literate and undersized (hence his nickname, 'the dillen' or runt) he possessed an extraordinary gift: he was a story-teller of genius in the old oral tradition. The tale he tells is *his* tale, and the tale of those he met from the 1870s to the aftermath of the Great War, recorded by his grandson's wife as he approached his hundredth year.

'a Warwickshire Decameron' *New Society*

'It is funny and heartbreaking by turn, packed with incidents and curiosities.' *Sunday Times*

'It takes the reader by the scruff of the neck and forces him to taste the food, smell the smells, agree to the tricks and breathe the air of a cheerful, dreadful England which would do for you if it could' *Ronald Blythe*

A COUNTRY CALENDAR AND
OTHER WRITINGS

Flora Thompson

Selected and edited by Margaret Lane

Illustrated by Clare Roberts

Admirers of Flora Thompson will welcome this volume of her writings selected and edited from her uncollected or unpublished papers. It includes Margaret Lane's biographical essay; *Heatherley,* a lightly disguised account of Flora Thompson's life in Grayshott, Hampshire before she married; a selection of her observations and other writings; some of her poems; and photographs and line drawings.

'A must for Flora Thompson addicts and a superb introduction to the uninitiated.' *The Times*

BLUE REMEMBERED HILLS

A Recollection

Rosemary Sutcliff

Rosemary Sutcliff is one of our most widely acclaimed novelists for children (and she has many adult admirers too). In *Blue Remembered Hills* she gives a moving account of the influences and the people that helped in her personal development as a writer.

'It is a remarkable book, not only for the clarity of her memory and for her determination to be honest, however painful the revelation, but also for her considerable powers of description' Caroline Moorehead in *The Times*